Difference
MAKING A

We could not have written this book without the dedication
of so many others who laid the foundation and contributed to building
this PreK–3 grade system. Thank you to all who helped us in this process,
trained with us, and continue to enrich the lives of children.

Linda dedicates this book to her husband, Tom; to their children, Serene and Jordan; to
extended family; and to the many children, families, and colleagues who have paved the
way and committed their lives to this important work. Every life has meaning
and a purpose, and I am thankful for your courage to put your individual
interests aside and stand up for our children.

Donna dedicates this book to her husband, Ron, and sons, Howard and Eric.
Their support and encouragement has made this dream a reality. Thank you to the
directors, teachers, and colleagues who have participated in trainings and welcomed me
into your classrooms and homes. Your work and passion for children are truly
making a difference in the lives of children.

Kelli dedicates this book to her husband, Aaron, their two sons, Kellen and Corbin, and
her extended family. This book would not have become a reality without your patience, support, and
forgiveness for the long hours spent on research and writing. I would also like to thank the leaders
and educators both in the Bremerton School District and in districts across the country that
I have had the opportunity to work with. Your dedication to the educational
profession and to the children you teach is inspiring.

MAKING A Difference

10 Essential Steps to Building a PreK–3 System

Linda Sullivan-Dudzic
Donna K. Gearns
Kelli Leavell
Foreword by **Ruby Takanishi**

CORWIN
A SAGE Company

For information:

Corwin
A SAGE Company
2455 Teller Road
Thousand Oaks, California 91320
(800) 233-9936
Fax: (800) 417-2466
www.corwinpress.com

SAGE India Pvt. Ltd.
B 1/I 1 Mohan Cooperative
    Industrial Area
Mathura Road, New Delhi 110 044
India

SAGE Ltd.
1 Oliver's Yard
55 City Road
London EC1Y 1SP
United Kingdom

SAGE Asia-Pacific Pte. Ltd.
33 Pekin Street #02-01
Far East Square
Singapore 048763

Printed in the United States of America

Library of Congress Cataloging-in-Publication Data

Sullivan-Dudzic, Linda.
Making a difference: 10 essential steps to building a preK-3 system/Linda Sullivan-Dudzic, Donna K. Gearns, Kelli Leavell; foreword by Ruby Takanishi.
        p. cm.
Includes bibliographical references and index.
ISBN 978-1-4129-7423-3 (pbk.: alk. paper)
    1. Early childhood education. I. Gearns, Donna K. II. Leavell, Kelli. III. Title.

LB1139.23.S85 2010
372.21—dc22   2009037010

This book is printed on acid-free paper.

09 10 11 12 13 10 9 8 7 6 5 4 3 2 1

Acquisitions Editor:	Jessica Allan
Associate Editor:	Joanna Coelho
Production Editor:	Amy Schroller
Copy Editor:	Mark Bast
Typesetter:	C&M Digitals (P) Ltd.
Proofreader:	Ellen Howard
Indexer:	Kirsten Kite
Cover Designer:	Rose Storey

Contents

Foreword

Since the 1970s, the United States has not only lost its standing as the country with the highest rates of college graduation in the world, it is also a country where K–12 educational achievement remains stubbornly stable at less than globally competitive levels. These basic facts are profoundly disturbing for a democracy that values individual achievement and effort as the path to a good life.

Educational success remains the path by which Americans improve their economic status from one generation to the next. Getting on that path begins early in life, even prenatally. Thus, policymakers and others focus on the critical importance of the early years in a child's life and the role that families play in being the child's "first teachers." However, since the end of the Second World War, American children now spend more time outside the home in a wide variety of family child care homes, Head Start, and prekindergarten (PreK) programs. States are beginning to recognize the value of quality PreK programs in contributing to the educational success of children.

These programs vary in their educational quality, and few are connected with the K–12 educational system. Typically there is a gap between the early childhood and the K–12 education systems that is inefficient and acts to obstruct the creation of a seamless continuum of learning for children from prekindergarten to kindergarten through third grade (PreK–3). As a result, even gains from quality PreK programs can fade out when children encounter poor quality elementary grade classrooms.

In what I call "a movement from the base"—a movement among educators in schools and in school districts—this gap is being closed through the thoughtful, innovative, and deep commitment of individuals who care about the educational success of all of America's children. Whether in Bremerton (Washington) or in Montgomery County (Maryland) or in First School (North Carolina), educators are showing that it is possible to put children—especially children who come from immigrant, low-income, or working-class families or are racial/ethnic minorities who do not typically experience good education—on a firm path to a college education and to opportunities for a good life in our country.

The authors are such educators who worked on connecting their K–12 school district, specifically grades K–3, with the community-based centers serving young children before kindergarten entry, starting in 2000. They did so, because they had a clear goal of increasing the educational achievement of the children in Bremerton. They succeeded. They write from direct experience combined with the ability to reflect on what they have learned and to share it with their colleagues so that many more children can benefit from what they accomplished.

How did they achieve what has eluded the vast majority of school districts in the United States, specifically those that have high rates of underachievement among their students? The answers to this most significant challenge facing American education are offered in this book in a clear, engaging, and useful manner. The lessons learned are ones that I have seen in other school districts and schools throughout the country that successfully integrate their early learning/PreK programs with their K–12 systems and have results to show for it. It is not rocket science. It is the plain hard work of creating an educational experience based on what works.

Here is how it can happen. Leadership—whether a superintendent or a principal—is key to articulating a focused goal of increasing the numbers of children who successfully complete their PreK–12 education. That individual, including being an instructional leader, must navigate through the normal political thicket that is part of any school district.

A team of dedicated, patient educators with their eyes on the prize and respect for all they work with, especially community members and staff in early learning programs, must work well with the leader to create a shared sense of purpose exemplified in joint professional development between the PreK and the K–3 staff working together on a common, aligned curriculum, which is democratically chosen. Instruction is constantly informed by data—what children are learning—and instruction is modified based on ongoing assessments of children's progress. Accountability is a hallmark and results are widely shared.

Every child can succeed, if more educators understood what it takes to create schools and districts where children can thrive. Such schools and districts begin with full-day prekindergarten and kindergarten programs that are laser-focused on instruction and learning. These schools use a standards-based curriculum, supported by shared professional development, shared diagnostic assessments, and shared accountability between educators and families. The entire effort is disciplined and data-driven.

To my knowledge, this is the first ever book to be written for educators on the path to implementing PreK–3 approaches. As more policymakers and educators see the value of these approaches, and they will, this book will pave the way to high quality and thoughtful implementation. The specificity and clarity of what needs to be done will be useful to those who have day-to-day responsibility for students. This is a guide written by their colleagues, who have walked the talk.

If we can get more schools and districts on this path, America will regain its entire educational leadership role. That time cannot come too soon.

Ruby Takanishi
President, Foundation for Child Development
New York City
May 2009

Acknowledgments

The authors would like to thank Jessica Allan, first for her belief in us and this project, then for her assistance, guidance, and words of wisdom throughout this process.

In addition, Corwin gratefully acknowledges the contributions of the following reviewers:

Sue Haas
Kindergarten Teacher
Big Bend School
Big Bend, WI

Brenda Hood
Special Assistant to the State Superintendent
Office of Superintendent of Public Instruction
Olympia, WA

Cindy Luna
NAESP 2004 National Distinguished Principal
Northside ISD
Texas Elementary Principal's Association
San Antonio, TX

Ganna Maymind
First-Grade Teacher
Asher Holmes Elementary School
Morganville, NJ

Wilma Robles-Melendez, PhD
Program Professor of Early Childhood Education
Nova Southeastern University
North Miami Beach, FL

Patti Ulshafer
First-Grade Teacher
Wilson Borough Elementary School
Easton, PA

Sally Wingle
Preschool Teacher
Chelsea Community Preschool, Chelsea School District
Chelsea, MI

About the Authors

 **Linda Sullivan-Dudzic, MSEd,** has spent the past 30 years connecting the years from early childhood through Grades K–12 to the higher education system. Prior to entering the fields of speech language pathology, curriculum and instruction, special education, and Title I, she learned a great deal from her mother, Lillian Sullivan, who started one of the first quality preschool programs in the 60s, The Julie Ann Nursery School, which included students with disabilities. Built on this strong early foundation, Linda continued her educational training and experience as a speech language pathologist at Kitsap Community Resources Head Start and started one of the first cooperative public school and Head Start service agreements to serve children with disabilities. Linda's advocacy for early childhood education and students with disabilities continued with her work with the public school system (birth to 12th grade) as a special programs director, as well as with her work in higher education designing and teaching college level courses, and finally, with her work with others to create a faith-based private preschool whose mission is to provide quality education to families who cannot afford preschool.

It is her hope that this book will benefit people who have dedicated their lives to the children and families they serve. Linda and her husband, Tom, have had their lives enriched by their two children, Serene and Jordan.

Donna K. Gearns, MSEd, began her teaching careerin self-contained preschool, elementary, and middle-school classrooms for students with learning disabilities. As an itinerant special education teacher, she discovered the importance of building relationships with staff and directors in community preschool settings, a critical step in the process of developing a PreK–3 grade system. Her work in quality preschool classrooms and collaboration with committed teachers and directors allowed her the opportunity to facilitate the use of common curriculum and its implementation in community preschool settings. Donna currently is a teacher on special assignment (TOSA) for Bremerton School District. In addition to working with community preschool programs, she is an assistive technology specialist for students from preschool through high school. Her goal is to make a difference for children and teachers by providing resources, information, and support. Donna and her husband have two sons and live with their three dogs in Seabeck, Washington.

Kelli Leavell started her career working as a special education teacher in the Bremerton School District. After several years in the classroom, she took her current position as a part-time district teacher on special assignment (TOSA). As a TOSA, Kelli has had the opportunity to coordinate the district English language learner program. She also provides coaching and training focused on districtwide initiatives like Response to Intervention, Title I services, reading instruction and alignment, and classroom management. Kelli also helps coordinate several grants in partnership with state and private foundations. In addition to her work as a TOSA, Kelli is also a national independent reading consultant. Over the last seven years, this role has allowed her to work with a multitude of wonderful schools and districts across the nation. She is currently working on a degree in education leadership to earn her administrative credential. Her goal is to continue to help districts connect, align, and improve education services for all children. Kelli and her husband, Aaron, reside in Silverdale, Washington, with their two sons, Kellen and Corbin.

Introduction: Connecting Early Childhood and K–12 Programs

How to Build a PreK–3 System

It is with great joy and hope that we write this book for those who have the passion and desire to connect early childhood programs with the K–3 system in order to increase achievement for all children. The joy comes from the assurance that if you build a strong PreK–3 system of support, children will benefit greatly. The hope comes from the knowledge that you can do the work of combining efforts to build a community-based support system that leads to higher gains for our young students.

We wrote this book for principals, administrators, school board members, and early childhood education directors and practitioners who are passionate about early learning. Providing a high-quality educational foundation starts children on the path toward academic success and multiple possibilities for a bright future. People who want to strengthen their efforts to build a PreK–3 system by adding broad-based support, community engagement, and financial stability realize they cannot do this work in isolation. Resources are difficult to secure and the needs of families and children are increasing. Connecting early childhood programs with the K–12 educational system is a proactive strategic plan to increase student achievement. Combining and maximizing every available resource, prioritizing your learning needs, and unifying your efforts to provide children with the early-foundation skills and academic instruction they require will have a lasting positive impact on the children in your community.

The question of whether or not to provide children with a high-quality education has been answered with a resounding yes from the field of early childhood research. The question of whether we should invest early to save remedial education and health and social services resources on the other end has also been answered in the affirmative. The question is not: "Should we connect our early childhood and K–12 communities to build a PreK–3 system?" The real question is *how* to do this. The authors have spent the past few decades learning how to connect early childhood programs with the K–12 system. We expanded our work to the larger community and recorded a systematic approach. The steps presented in this book will save you time and will make a significant positive change for children.

Numerous statistics keep us up at night and confirm the need for PreK–3 intervention. The United States has the largest per capita prison population in the world (Pew Study, 2008). Sixty percent of America's prison inmates are illiterate and 85 percent of all juvenile offenders have reading problems (National Adult Literacy Survey, 1992). The cost of illiteracy to businesses and taxpayers is $20 billion per year ("Illiteracy: A National Crisis," United Way). The Committee for Economic Development found that investing $4,800 per child in preschool could reduce teenage arrest by 40 percent (Carroll, 2008). Just as compelling is the growing body of research that confirms the significant impact we make when children receive quality early education aligned with quality K–3 education. It is no wonder that there is a renewed energy around early learning across our nation. President Barack Obama's State of the Economy speech, on April 14, 2009, included these words:

> But in this new economy, we've come to trail the world's leaders in graduation rates, in educational achievement, and production of scientists and engineers. That's why we have set a goal that will greatly enhance our ability to compete for the high-wage, high-tech jobs of the 21st century. By 2020, America will once again have the highest proportion of college graduates in the world. That is the goal that we have set and we intend to meet. To meet that goal, we have to start early. We have dramatically expanded early childhood education; we are investing in innovative programs that have proven to help schools meet high standards and close achievement gaps.

With early learning as a top priority, many of us are engaged in conversations about the hopeful possibilities. There is a willingness on the part of both the preschool and the K–12 communities to work together. Currently, thirty-three states are looking at a PreK–age 16 or PreK–age 20 initiative as a way to increase student achievement. Ruby Takanishi and Kristie Kauerz stated,

> Aligning early childhood education with elementary schools is not a new idea. Since initiatives in the early 1970s to connect Head Start with elementary schools, such as Project Follow Through and Project Development Continuity, a few policy makers and educators have tried to bridge that gap between the culture of early education and K–12 education. They considered that one or two years of early childhood education would not be sufficient to sustain gains in achievement over the long term. For low-income children, sustaining the gains made as a result of attending high-quality prekindergarten programs requires continuing to provide them with high-quality learning experiences into the elementary school years (Takanishi & Kauerz, 2008).

We have referenced our work in the Bremerton School District as well as other examples of success stories across the nation to demonstrate what can happen when early childhood programs and K–12 public schools unite. For those of you who have already developed a community-based PreK–3 system, we encourage you to read through each chapter, finding validation in what you have already accomplished and making note of what may be helpful to enhance your system or broaden your base of support to increase student achievement. Upon completion of this book, you may want to go back and use it as a resource to review, revise, and extend your system.

The following steps are arranged in sequential order for people like us who want to know where we are going and how to get there.

Step 1: Establish Need and Common Interests. This is the first step to bringing your community together. It starts by having you take a critical look at the educational needs of the children you serve and comparing them to national data and trends. While acknowledging the work that has been done thus far, you will gather current research and information to share with your group to establish a common level of understanding and ground your efforts.

Step 2: Connect With Your Early Childhood Learning Environments. We will walk you through a process of locating your community preschool partners and enable you to navigate your way through the world of early childhood education. Practical location strategies are provided to get all stakeholders at your first PreK–3 meeting. A helpful outline for the first meeting that ends with a commitment and established goals is provided.

Step 3: Develop a Leadership Group. This step will show you how to gather representatives from the preschool and K–12 environments who are committed to your established goals. It provides a simplified plan with accompanied activities to establish a culture of inquiry and respectful problem solving. Procedures for reaching agreements, establishing common curriculum, and ensuring assessments that support your goals and measure your progress are provided.

Step 4: High-Quality Professional Development. Included here are practical strategies and a format to use with your providers to create monthly professional development. Step 4 presents meaningful application of research, hands-on activities, and strategies to meet the needs of a wide range of adult learners.

Step 5: Connect and Align Quality PreK to Kindergarten. Here we provide the next steps to move the very best of a quality preschool foundation up to elementary school and also the strengths of a K–12 system down to preschool. Important parts of this step are how to align early learning benchmarks (standards) with K–3 state standards, how to develop and align a strong assessment and information loop, and how to align curriculum and instructional practices that support children's learning. Also in this section is how to build PreK–3 or PreK–5 elementary schools and the role of the principals.

Step 6: Maximize the Benefits of Full-Day Kindergarten. This step is full of practical strategies and sequential components to build a strong instructional program. It will illustrate how to establish agreements on the best instructional practices and support systems to use districtwide. Information is also included on how principals and their instructional-leadership team utilize assessment data to inform instruction.

Step 7: Align and Connect a Strong Full-Day Kindergarten With Grades 1–3. Here we take the process outlined in Step 5 and apply key concepts to use for Grades 1–3. This alignment provides an important foundational component needed prior to Step 8 to prevent fade-out.

Step 8: Conquer the Fade-Out. This step looks at current research and recommendations to ensure that your documented success and the benefits to children from your preschool efforts do not fade. It will guide your group through a planning process to ensure that you are keeping a watchful eye on every child, adjusting and modifying the curriculum as children continue through the grades. It also provides strategies to align vertically, horizontally, temporally, and more. Your group will formulate a plan from the start to make certain that your system is strong enough to conquer the fade-out.

Step 9: Create a Sustainable System of Support. Outlined here are the critical components to finance and sustain your PreK–3 system of support. A dynamic PreK–3 system is one that continues to respond to the needs of the children in your community. We suggest ways to build broad-based support, recruit and engage community partners, and plan for financial stability.

Step 10: Review, Revise, and Extend. Just when you thought you were done, you realize that these same steps allow you to revise and expand your system of support. Examples are provided on how to extend to in-home providers and expand to higher education. Step 10 will provide considerations for building a PreK–16 system and beyond.

One of the greatest joys of working with so many passionate and talented people for so many years is experiencing on a daily basis the positive impact quality education and instruction have on the lives of children and families. With joy and hope also comes a sense of urgency and accountability for the children under our watch. Because we have seen the encouraging effects of high-quality PreK–3 grade systems on children in many communities, in addition to the discouraging effects and the dismal, lasting impact of substandard early learning environments and poor instruction, we can no longer settle for mediocrity. We stand firm in our belief that you cannot increase student achievement with isolated efforts of excellence. It takes a community-based team effort to build a dynamic PreK–3 system that continues to expand and respond to the needs of all children. We believe that you need both a top-down (policies and allocated funding) as well as a bottom-up (community-based efforts using existing resources) approach to accomplish this work. Our goal is to help as many local communities, states, and federal organizations as possible so that this hope becomes a reality and life-changing opportunity for children everywhere.

Step 1

Establish Need and Common Interests

Connecting to Your Preschool Community

Have you ever felt overwhelmed by the needs of your community? Have you served on multiple committees that began as a collaborative effort only to find your efforts stymied by competing needs and lack of focus? Are you living in a community where poverty is on the rise and funding is dwindling? The negative talk and criticism of public education is enough to drag down the most positive person. It does not have to be that way. Without the entire community, no school district is able to provide children with the necessary early learning skills required to be successful in life. We define *early learning* as that critical period of child development, from birth to age eight, and the *early learning community* as all adults and agencies that touch the lives of young children and families. Step 1 presents information to establish a joint effort between local and state educational institutions (the K–12 public school system) and a mix of early childhood (PreK) providers to work toward a common goal. The goal is to increase the quality of early childhood education (PreK–3). This system provides a strong early childhood foundation prior to kindergarten and builds upon and extends quality education during the kindergarten through third grade (K–3) years, resulting in significant improvements in the lives of children.

We offer a series of community- and strength-based strategies to bring your preschool community and K–3 system together to focus on the needs of children. You may want to pause and ask yourself: Do you believe children's lives (and our own world) significantly improve when children receive quality learning environments during the PreK–3 years? Do you believe the adults must take the responsibility to provide the instructional program and teach skills necessary for all children to reach their full potential?

Across our nation, children continue to spend time in impoverished early learning environments followed by inadequate public education. In the past, our poor families suffered the most, many times having to choose between quality programs and affordability. Now, our middle-class families have joined them in being the recipients of the negative effects of poor-quality early education. W. Steven Barnett, Board of Governors, professor, and codirector of the National Institute for Early Education Research at Rutgers University reveals that

> the number of middle-class children with cognitive test scores below the average for poor children at kindergarten entry exceeds the number of poor children who score this low. Subsequently, nearly one in 10 middle-class children repeats a grade and the same percentage drop out of high school (Barnett, 2008).

Even when a child experiences a rich educational preschool environment, valuable learning time is lost because we do not align our K–3 instruction and fail to build upon the strong foundational skills provided at the preschool level. The negative consequences of a disjointed PreK–3 system are often irreversible and impact the next generation.

You may be thinking at this point, I would love to build a PreK–3 unified approach to teaching and learning, but I don't have the resources. Take heart because we will offer multiple ways to fund your efforts using existing resources. Often, a lack of resources can be a catalyst to building systems. When resources are scarce, such circumstances compel us to look at entire programs and services to children. Ask the questions: What are we doing that is effective? Are there any redundancies? and Are our instructional practices having a lasting impact on the children we serve? The focus shifts from individual crisis intervention to examining your entire community, district, and schoolwide system.

Examine the following steps and adapt them for your community. Remember, stay focused on the needs of your children and what they require for a brighter future. This is not a choice between providing children with a nurturing environment to develop social skills *or* with a strong early childhood skill foundation (vocabulary, oral language, math, reading, science, and writing). We do not have the luxury to pick and choose what to teach. Armed with the most current research on how young children learn, and aware of the critical components necessary to teach, we can all agree that our children need it all.

Connecting the Early Childhood Community and K–12 Public Schools

Gather Current Research and Establish Need

It is important to ground your collective efforts in research and the needs of children. Gather current research and information to share with your PreK–3 groups to establish a common level of understanding and create an environment of inquiry. A respectful examination of new information facilitates the discussion and is more productive than reexamining old practices and opinions on how children should be taught. Here are a few important facts that we have found helpful in mobilizing preschool community efforts. We have used these in handouts, PowerPoint presentations, and "Did you know?" talking points to let preschool providers know how important their work is and why we need to join efforts.

- "The opportunity to attend a quality PreK class makes a child 40 percent less likely to need special education services, 40 percent less likely to repeat a grade, and twice as likely to attend college" (*Patrick*, 2007). The key is quality education. This again underscores the need to define *quality* in your PreK–3 system.

- The reverse is also true; our nation pays a significant price for inadequate education in terms of income, health care, crime, and dependence on public assistance (Levin & Belfield, 2007). What are the implications for children who start behind? Two out of every five students receiving special education in the United States were identified because of difficulties in learning to read (EdPubs 2002).

- Recently, many states have discovered that despite their best efforts to provide quality preschool instruction, the benefits start to fade after first grade. Both Ruby Takanishi and Kristie Kauerz have done extensive work in this area and have provided valuable information

(Takanishi & Kauerz, 2008). A critical step to providing a sustainable PreK–3 system is to align instruction.

Expanding Beyond the Public-School Preschool Model to Reach More Children

In response to the urgent need to increase the number of children entering kindergarten with strong foundational skills, some school districts and states have created district-sponsored preschool programs. A district-run preschool offers several advantages, including the implementation of school district curriculum, certified teachers, no cost or low cost to families, and smooth transitions. Some disadvantages are a significant reduction in the number of children served and the potential loss of shared resources and revenue to community preschools and child care programs.

We advocate for lifting up your entire early childhood community. Work with all preschools in your community using a mixed model: Head Start, state-owned, community, faith-based, and in-home child care providers. In our work with a number of early learning preschool providers with a variety of backgrounds and formal education, we know that when you treat preschool providers with respect and furnish the research and tools they require, combined with job-embedded professional development, the results yield positive documented outcomes for children. This gives families expanded options, and more children receive early learning support. When school districts are not paying the cost of preschool operations, they are able to extend their other resources, such as professional development, curriculum materials, and assessments, to community preschools.

Establishing Need and Prioritizing Your PreK–3 Efforts

What Are Your Reasons?

Take a moment right now and list all the reasons why this effort is so important and why you need the help of everyone in your community. For us, with a background in special education, it was personal and very basic; when children enter kindergarten behind, very few ever recover. Add that to current research in learning disabilities associated with reading and math emphasizing the importance of early intervention and need for research-based instruction (Fletcher, Lyon, Fuchs, & Barnes, 2007), the importance of vocabulary and background knowledge (Marzano, 2004), and the fact that quality preschool makes a significant difference in the future of our children.

We, like many of you, believe we have a moral obligation to help all children in our community. In our work, we found that not every kindergarten through third-grade classroom is of high quality, and not every preschool is a place where you would enroll your own child. What are the realities in your state or community? Think about equity and access. Are there high-quality preschools and examples of aligned preschool and kindergarten efforts that you wish you could replicate or extend? Are there children arriving at the door of kindergarten lacking foundational skills and continuing on a downward educational path? Look at your own children, ask the questions, and call for a unified community effort. Establishing the needs of your children, PreK–3, and a commitment to respectful dialog are your first steps to establishing a PreK–3 system.

Your First Early Childhood and K–3 Meeting

The next step is to connect with and invite your community preschool providers to a PreK–3 meeting. The group that you invite will become your leadership group. This group will look at the critical skills needed for children to enter kindergarten with higher-level foundational skills and will select one or two priority goals to work on and problem-solve together. Right up front, it is important to convey to the preschool community how much you need their help and what a difference they make in the lives of children.

Narrowing Your Focus

To build your PreK–3 system of support, you will need to start with one or two skills that both the early childhood and K–3 teachers agree are important for children to learn and demonstrate with greater proficiency. You want to even the playing field where both systems serve an important role in the child's skill development. One suggestion is to start with social and emotional skills, as well as reading skills.

An examination of how children learn and the best PreK–3 instructional practices using current brain and early literacy research is a great place to start. Carol Cummings does an excellent job in her book, *Winning Strategies*, of pulling together the brain research on how children learn and their social and emotional needs for success with the need to teach skills. She states that one of the ways we can increase these expectations for success is by teaching the skills necessary to perform the task (Cummings, 2000). In the area of reading, early childhood and K–3 play a critical role in phonological awareness, phonics, vocabulary, language development, fluency, and comprehension. Providing the following materials at your first meeting and having them available for review and discussion, as well as other current references, will build the background knowledge necessary for your first meeting and the work of this group:

- The report *Developing Early Literacy: Report of the National Early Literacy Panel* (2008) covers the importance and the essentials of teaching early reading. It is a free National Institute for Literacy publication.

- *Foundations for Success: The Final Report of the National Mathematics Advisory Panel* (U.S. Department of Education, 2008) contains essential components of math instruction and stresses the importance of teaching early math.

- *Nurturing Knowledge: Building a Foundation for School Success by Linking Early Literacy to Math, Science, Art, and Social Studies* (Neuman, Roskos, Wright, & Lenhart, 2007) combines both early childhood research and practice.

- *Brain-Friendly Strategies for the Inclusion Classroom: Insights From a Neurologist and Classroom Teacher* (Willis, 2007) discuses the optimal learning and teaching environment.

- *12 Brain/Mind Principles in Action: Developing Executive Functions of the Human Brain* (Caine, Caine, McClintic, & Klimek, 2009) provides teaching strategies based on neuroscience.

One quick way to select your shared target area(s) for your initial focus is to have your leadership group participate in a selection process. Ask all participants at your first meeting to list all of the developmental areas (skills) that they directly work on (teach) at each grade: preschool, kindergarten, first, second, and third. Circle or combine areas that are similar, continue through third grade, and have a significant impact on student learning. This activity will not be necessary if your community has already established a primary focus. Your next step will be to reinforce this by establishing specific needs and areas of focus.

National Data

We have provided the following statistics that you can share with your community. These national statistics call us to action. Examine the following data and make these into a PowerPoint presentation or handout. To establish your need, share these facts and questions with your leadership group at your first meeting (*Reading Reality*, 1998):

Figure 1.1 Children Entering Kindergarten

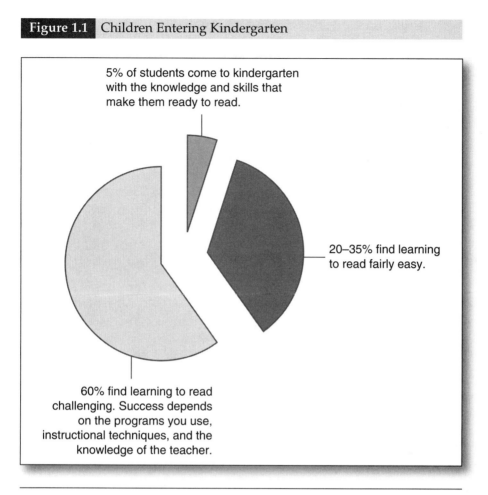

5% of students come to kindergarten with the knowledge and skills that make them ready to read.

20–35% find learning to read fairly easy.

60% find learning to read challenging. Success depends on the programs you use, instructional techniques, and the knowledge of the teacher.

Source: National Center for Education Statistics (2006)

- Many children find learning how to read very difficult. Children require the help of knowledgeable teachers; all will benefit from a research-based curriculum that provides the greatest probability of success.
- 5 percent of students come to kindergarten with the knowledge and skills that make them ready to read.
- 20–35 percent find learning to read fairly easy.
- 60 percent find learning to read challenging. Success depends on the programs you use, instructional techniques, and the knowledge of the teacher.
- What are the implications for children who do not receive quality early childhood instruction? When children start behind, many children stay behind despite heroic educational efforts. When children enter kindergarten with strong foundation

skills, their options expand and their futures have many positive possibilities. Children who are below reading-benchmark skill levels by the end of first grade have a one in four to one in seven chance of catching up without intensive and costly intervention (Simmons, Coyne, Kwok, McDonagh, Harn, & Kame'enui, 2008).

• Which children are most likely to struggle? Children in poverty and children at risk for learning disabilities are in danger of needing additional intervention.

When sharing this first-meeting information, it is important to read the Hart and Risley (1995) study. This study focuses on American children's family experiences, their socioeconomic status, and the implications for vocabulary development. Be sure to emphasize to your community that the difference in interactive words is not due to a lack of love or interest on the part of low-income families. These families are often struggling by trying to support their families and as a result, use language that is more directive and shorter in length. For example, if a child has fewer options for shoes, parents will use fewer adjectives to describe the shoes they want their child to put on. This difference continues well into elementary grades, as illustrated below.

| Figure 1.2 | Beginning Kindergartners' School-Readiness by Socioeconomic Status (SES) | |

	Lowest SES	Highest SES
Recognizes letters of alphabet	39%	85%
Identifies beginning sounds of words	10%	51%
Identifies primary colors	69%	90%
Counts to 20	48%	68%
Writes own name	54%	76%

	Lowest SES	Highest SES
Amount of time having been read to prior to kindergarten	25 hours	1,000 hours
Total number of words heard	13 million	45 million

Sources: Lee & Burkam, 2002; Adams, 1990; National Center for Education Statistics, 2000; Neuman, 2003; Hart & Risley 1995.

Figure 1.3 Socioeconomic status is the greatest predictor of academic success.

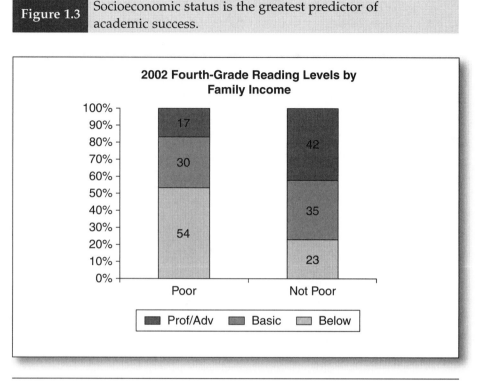

Source: National Center for Education Statistics (2006)

Local Data

Next, gather and examine your own data to look at the specific needs of the children in your community. Check for the following:

- Poverty level
- Number of children who qualify for free and reduced-cost lunch
- Mobility rate
- Number of available preschools in the area
- Number of Head Start programs and availability
- Number of children attending preschool
- Number of children who do not attend preschool
- Remedial budgets and compensatory services (Title I, special education)
- Achievement trend data

How does your community compare with national-trend data? What is the cost of trying to remediate deficits in your school district? Are you using measures that are comparable nationwide? To increase the quality of our programs and instructional practices, we need to be willing to use measures that compare our children to children across the nation. It is important that you are clear on the intent of gathering this form of assessment data and that you include your community preschools in discussions regarding the need for, and the use of, these data. The assessment you choose is not to identify children for special education or to make placement decisions at the individual child level. Assessments that are more comprehensive are required when making high-stakes decisions for children. These assessment data are used to measure progress on your target outcomes and to improve your instruction (system of support).

At the time of publication, we still do not have quick comprehensive measures for children that meet all our needs in the area of assessment. Choose from what is available to give your group consistent feedback as to how your children are doing. Without this local data, you will not be able to go to your community and ask that they examine their own practices to create a PreK–3 system of support. If we want to increase the quality of instruction in our learning environments, we must be willing to add to our repertoire the ability to gather useful assessment data aligned to our goals.

Many states and school districts use the following individual assessments:

- Dynamic Inventory of Basic Early Literacy Skills (DIBELS)
- Get It Got It Go, for preschool literacy assessment
- AIMS Web for math and literacy
- Devereaux Early Childhood Assessment Program (DECA) for social and emotional assessment
- Florida Assessments for Instruction in Reading, Florida Center for Reading Research

These measures will give you a universal screening indicator to let you know if children are at risk and need more targeted practice opportunities. Many states, including Washington, have early childhood assessment documents that may help you select a universal screener to administer to your preschool and kindergarten children if you have not done so in the past. One excellent free resource is *Washington State: A Guide to Assessment in Early Childhood Infancy to Age Eight* (Slentz, Early, & McKenna, 2008). See Resource A for more information.

When we looked at our own local data, we had to admit that our children and families struggled with the same risk factors, and our outcome data [were] consistent with national trends. In fact, it was a shock to find out that despite our successful efforts in the area of social and emotional needs and our work with our early childhood providers on integrating special education students, our students came to kindergarten woefully behind. Be willing to admit to your community the fact that when your children start kindergarten behind, it is very difficult for them to catch up. The more children that enter kindergarten behind, the more resources that are needed to provide the intensive support these children require to develop basic skills. Approach your early childhood community to look at your need, respectfully examine data, and establish mutual goals. Your initial contacts and first meeting are critical for establishing a climate of inquiry, mutual respect, and problem solving.

STEP 1 AT A GLANCE

- Gather research and information to share with your PreK–3 group to establish a common level of understanding and to ground your efforts.
- Take a moment to list the reasons that compel you to unite with your early childhood community. These reasons make a difference now in the lives of children and families in your community.
- Acknowledge the fact that children are your priority and create a culture of mutual respect for all PreK–3 staff and families around this common theme.
- Make a decision to include all community providers to lift up the quality of education for all children.
- Gather information for your first early childhood (PreK) and K–12 meeting.
- Establish the need and prioritize your PreK–3 efforts.
- Narrow your focus.
- Gather national and local data to present at your first meeting.

Next Step: Connect with and invite your community preschool providers to a PreK–3 meeting. The group that you invite will become your PreK–3 leadership group.

Step 2

Locate and Connect With Your Early Childhood Learning Environments

Of course, people cannot contribute to the nation if they are never taught to read or write, if their bodies are stunted from hunger, if their sickness goes untended, if their life is spent in hopeless poverty just drawing a welfare check.

—Lyndon B. Johnson, Message to Congress:
The American Promise, March 15, 1965

President Lyndon Johnson's War on Poverty created the federal Head Start preschool program for children and families in poverty. Its intent was to bridge the achievement gap by addressing the needs of the whole child, including the need for a firm foundation in early academic skills. This same movement created the Title I federal academic program to address the academic needs of low-income K–12 students in our public schools. Title I alone spent over $120 billion to create a complex web of K–12 educational services (Mead, 2007).

After 45 years, it appears that we are no further along in our efforts to connect these two, as well as other effective programs, to create a PreK–3 system of support. In hindsight, we set ourselves up by creating two separate federal programs that have the same vision and target the same children and families. Your job is to bring these two programs and other preschool and K–3 efforts together to expand the benefits to all children. Who in your state or community is in charge of your Title I and Head Start programs? These two departments will need to work closely together. They are your first potential unifying funding streams. Both Title I and Head Start have received additional funding from the American Recovery and Reinvestment Act of 2009. These funds are to be used to drive school reform and improvement. Both Title I and Head Start have a mandate to reach across to connect with the other (transition); a requirement to raise achievement and demonstrate early academic (reading and math) outcomes. To support these mandates, each program provides funding and requirements in the area of highly qualified teachers and professional development. As you know, alignment of funding is just the beginning to putting an end to fragmented services; the real work is to bring your community preschools together with your K–3 public school to unify and align your efforts to build a high-quality system of support.

The good news is that more public school districts are opening their doors to Head Start and other preschool to share facilities, increasing the possibility of collaboration. However, few have capitalized on this arrangement and made the preschool program and staff an integral part of the school's effort to increase student achievement. Look around in your community. What are the possibilities? Who are your potential partners? The preschool and the K–12 educational systems are comprised of multiple levels of services and supports that offer tremendous potential (Preschool Special Education Part C, Early Head Start, Migrant Head Start, Tribal Head Start, Title I, Title II Highly Qualified Teachers, special education, state and federal bilingual education). If unified, these programs and services are the building blocks of PreK–3 school reform. Even within the elementary schools, often young children move from one adult to the next, receiving a variety of special services from as many as eight different teachers and volunteers in a single day. Our children at risk in the preschool environment and those who are already behind in the K–3 environment deserve a better system of support. Connecting systems is an effective way to share resources and focus research-based instruction and the best practices to benefit children and families. This work is difficult, but it does not have to be so complicated. To quote a very dear friend of ours, Sandy Hendrickson, "Aren't we all here for the kids?"

Locate Your Community Preschool Partners

Do You Know Where Children Are Prior to Attending Your School District?

Who are the key people in your community that care for and teach the children who will enter your kindergartens? Invite them to a "kick-off" meeting, with the preschool providers meeting with the school district to talk about common needs and shared goals. How do you locate these individuals? Where do you start?

Start by publicly acknowledging that learning does not begin in kindergarten. This fact appears obvious to most, but there continue to be misconceptions on the part of some in both preschool and the K–12 system as to the importance and value of early education. This is largely due to the fact that the quality of programs and services vary in both the preschool and the K–12 system. For example, in community preschools, there are quality nurturing preschool environments that our public school system could learn from and others that may be well intentioned but are substandard, dismal preschool environments that stifle children's capacity for learning. Your job as a school district is to invite as many community preschools as possible. Your goal is to work with your community to raise the quality of instruction in your own school district and in all preschool environments. At this point, your ability to form a community-based PreK–3 effort is limited only by your ability to locate preschool providers, form a positive relationship with the school district, and establish a commitment and unified plan to increase achievement. Families choose their child care and preschool for a variety of reasons: quality, cost, convenience, faith, trust, a neighbor's recommendation, because their child has a disability, because a preschool has an excellent reputation for getting children ready for kindergarten, or a combination of these reasons. Start by asking the parents of your kindergarten children what the best preschools are in your community. Call these preschools and respectfully invite their owners and directors to the kick-off meeting. Let them know that you value the important work that they are doing and the relationship they have built with the families in your community.

Practical Ways to Locate Preschool Owners and Directors

The following are some practical ways to locate preschool owners and directors:

- Use your local early childhood resource and referral networks. Most states and many communities have established an early childhood care and education database and referral system.

- Gather information on preschools in your area from kindergarten registration forms. Use your district kindergarten registration form to create a database of the preschools children attend prior to kindergarten.
- Ask your teachers to identify preschools they trust and where their own children attended. Teachers are an excellent resource for finding preschools that excel at getting children "ready" for kindergarten.
- Invite your Head Start programs (including Tribal Head Start and Migrant Head Start) and state preschools.
- Ask your bus drivers and school secretaries to recommend preschools in the area.
- Check with your local health district and pediatricians.
- Advertise. Place an ad in the local newspaper. Display posters around your area. Ask the local community television channel to broadcast your early learning efforts.
- Post it on your district Web site.
- Create a flyer and post it throughout the community at places such as teacher supply stores, dollar stores, and grocery stores.
- Include faith-based preschools.

A Note on Faith-Based Preschools

Faith-based preschools reflect the values expressed in your community. Many of our community faith-based preschools reach out to low-income families by offering tuition assistance or sponsorship. Because these preschools are operating as a mission or outreach, they have their own unique strengths and challenges. Often they have financial hardships and difficulty with recruitment. Many lack the ability to access professional development. Often these preschools are required to hire within, and the pool of teacher applicants may be limited. One author has been blessed with the opportunity co-design and implement a quality faith-based preschool, Wonders of Learning, for the past 11 years. We established our agreements with the church from the start by establishing bylaws that enabled us to independently recruit, hire, and dismiss teaching staff. A research-validated early literacy curriculum is taught and overlaid on top of a Bible-based curriculum. The preschool works cooperatively with the local school district, including children with disabilities, offering multiple scholarships, and serving a wide range of socioeconomic families. Our preschool was voted number one by the local kindergarten teachers for providing an excellent early learning foundation for the children in that community. Without the strong connection to the school district, monthly professional development, and access to research-validated curriculum and materials, as well as excellent teachers, this preschool would still be struggling, with expectations no higher than providing a safe and nurturing environment. Wonders of Learning is an example of what can happen when, in this case, God intervenes and school districts and community preschools unite.

When faith-based preschools form a strong connection with your elementary schools and work with you to build a PreK–3 system of support, children and families benefit. The quality of early learning instruction for children is enhanced without asking families to sacrifice their own faith.

Identify and Locate Key People in Your School District

Every successful PreK–3 system has a strong leader at the administrative level and a leadership team to sustain the effort. Identify those people from the start and make them part of your leadership group. Create a strong PreK–3 system by obtaining the approval and support of your district superintendent and identifying individuals in key positions that who able to make districtwide decisions and commit resources. As you work together to increase the quality of early learning instruction (PreK–3), record and publicize your successful outcomes. The goal is to broaden your level of support and continue to expand the number of individuals throughout your school district and community who are knowledgeable about your work. Success builds on success: school boards, elected officials, businesses, and private funders all want to be part of positive outcomes for young children. Consider contacting the following people to move your PreK–3 system forward:

- Contact your local elementary-school principals.
- Contact your local kindergarten teachers.
- Invite parents. These are the people who are most invested in the outcome and who will keep the topic focused on the needs of children. Invite the parents who helped you locate and connect with your community preschools. Invite parents who have children with disabilities. Invite private-school parents and parents of Head Start children.
- Include a member of your school board for this initial meeting.
- Invite a central-office person (superintendent).
- Contact your school district's Title I director.
- Contact your school district's PTA president.

- Invite "champions" of child care issues in your community.
- Consider inviting higher-education personnel. They can provide a strong supportive role by providing teachers with solid knowledge-based and research-based instructional strategies for teaching young children.
- Consider other organizations and representative groups unique to your community (e.g., tribal or other cultural leaders).

Plan for Your Kick-Off PreK–3 Meeting

This meeting is a call to action; together we make a difference for the children in our community! "If you only sit around the table and wait for the state to fund it all, or some new insight to drop from the sky on how to do this, you're going to stall out" (Kettlewell, 2008).

Know that the people you have invited, those who are closest to the issue and work with children and families every day, have the greatest potential to make positive change. Create an atmosphere of excitement and anticipation about what might be possible if you joined together for the benefit of children.

Here are some helpful steps for your kick-off meeting. This meeting is critical to the establishment and success of your PreK–3 system of support. Your goal is to engage your community preschools in this effort.

At this kick-off meeting, you will do the following:

- Establish the need
- Create a culture of inquiry and problem solving
- Establish mutual goals with passion
- Name your group
- Set consistent meeting times

Choose a Facilitator

Choose a facilitator for this initial meeting, someone who is either neutral or, if possible, a "connector." A connector is someone who has established relationships in both the world of preschool and public education, who is respected and well known for putting children first. The facilitator must have the skills to encourage discussion as well as action. Create a professional atmosphere for adult learning. Provide handouts, research articles, and copies of your PowerPoint, or other, presentation so that participants go home with accurate information to share with others.

Suggested Format for Your Kick-Off Meeting

1. **Thank your preschools for all that they do for children and families.**

   Begin by saying something like this:

   We (the school districts) know that so much learning happens prior to kindergarten. We have brought you here to look at a national and local need shared by all adults working in the field of early childhood during the preschool through third-grade years. We know that together we can significantly change the lives of the children. We have a lot to learn from preschool, and we have some information to share with you as well.

2. **Proceed with introductions.**

   Have the participants go around the room and introduce themselves and answer two questions: Why do you love working with young children and families? and What do you want children to know and be able to do when they exit 12th grade?

3. **Create a presentation on the need for children to enter kindergarten with a strong developmental foundation followed by quality K–3 instruction.**

   Start with a few slides and cite national statistics on what happens when children start behind in kindergarten. Collect your own national research or use the information from Step 1. Follow up with local data and emphasize the fact that when children start behind, it is very difficult for them to catch up. Next, present the facts from Step 1 that make clear the difference a quality preschool makes in the lives of children. Talk about the research done on early reading skills and learning disabilities or math and the importance of vocabulary development. You can also include a few slides on brain development and the importance of providing multiple joyful practice opportunities. Pause to acknowledge preschools in your group and the fact that children are hungry to learn and far more capable than we (the public school system) ever realized. Talk about the fact that the greatest gains obtained for children occur when full-day kindergarten and quality K–3 instruction follow a high-quality preschool. Emphasize that much of the preschool efforts can be lost if not built on at the kindergarten level. Finally, pose this question: what are the possibilities if both the preschool and the K–3 system work together to provide the best instruction for all our children? What would that look like for our children when they graduate from high school? What are the possibilities that would be open to these children and the next generation of children? Divide into small mixed groups of no more than three to share your thoughts. Record the answers.

4. **Establish broad-based goals: vision plus action.**

   Foundational skills prior to kindergarten are so critical for success in life. Select only two goals; you cannot cover everything this first year. Some goal examples from our work are to increase the number of children entering

   (Continued)

(Continued)

kindergarten with foundational skills in reading and math and to decrease the number of children with learning difficulties associated with reading and math.

5. **Name your group and establish meeting times.**

Before you close the meeting, make sure you name the group and establish your next meeting time. This solidifies your group's commitment. Quickly choose a name that you can all live with. In our community, we called ourselves the Early Childhood Care and Education Group (ECCE). One community reported that they took so much time debating the name they ended up calling themselves NOG (Name of Group). Many organizations and committees lack the momentum and ability to move forward because they consistently revisit issues and change their direction when new players join the group. Once you have formed an agreement, you need to record it and move forward. There may be a tendency to build on an existing group or organization; it is important that you establish a new group, new goals, and shared power from the start.

6. **Send out follow-up announcements with your new name, meeting time, and goals.**

If possible, have your school board sign the announcements. Post these kick-off participants on your school district Web site. These are ways to build broad-based support and plan for sustainability.

STEP 2 AT A GLANCE

- Locate the preschools that children attend prior to kindergarten and invite the directors or owners to a PreK–3 meeting.
- Build on the strengths of your community. Problem-solve together and develop solutions. Relationships and mutual respect are key components to building a dynamic PreK–3 system of support.
- At the kick-off meeting, establish the need, create a culture of inquiry, develop mutual goals, name your group, and establish the next meeting time.
- Choose a facilitator and modify or follow the outline for your kick-off meeting.

Next Step: From this large gathering of committed individuals, you will develop a core leadership group (your school district and the early childhood PreK community) that will meet monthly to examine data, establish goals, select curriculum materials, design professional development, and measure your outcomes.

Step 3

Develop a Leadership Group

Michael Fullan has done extensive work on initiating change and school reform. He talks about the messiness of change and the tremendous potential for a positive outcome (Fullan, 2001). Most recently, Alan M. Blankstein, in his book *Failure Is Not an Option: Six Principles That Guide Student Achievement in High-Performing Schools*, talks about the difficulty that many encounter when attempting to build a professional learning community with relational trust: "Making fundamental changes and shifts in assumptions, beliefs, and actions is difficult. It is far easier to make slight modifications to old behaviors and then give the effort a new name" (Blankstein, 2004). This is so true in the complex world of systems development and specifically when attempting to cross the chasm between preschool and the K–3 educational programs. The encouraging news is that you can build an effective PreK–3system, focused on increasing achievement, by using a unified approach that honors existing efforts and builds on the strengths and resources in your community.

Your Leadership Group

Out of the participants from your community preschool and school district kick-off meeting outlined in Step 2, you will form your leadership group. Build a professional learning community within this group to take the goals you established (e.g., increasing the number of children entering kindergarten with early literacy skills and decreasing the number of children with learning disabilities associated with reading) and turn them into a reality for children. Your leadership group will be responsible for building the PreK–3 system of support that will provide your teachers and children with what they need to be successful. Members should include representatives from each community preschool and K–3 partner, parents, and at least one school district administrator who will champion this effort and be able to reallocate resources.

For the sake of providing concrete steps and relevant examples, we will focus primarily on the important skill of early literacy and how to build the knowledge base of your leadership group. It saddens us to note that while there is national interest and support for early learning, there continues to be opposition to teaching young children what they need to know prior to kindergarten in our field of early childhood. It often springs from misinformation on what is appropriate to teach and learn in early childhood. Why do we continue the debate regarding whether or not to teach social and emotional skills *or* early literacy? Obviously, we need to do it all and take pride in the fact that we (early childhood professionals) will prepare children for a brighter future. As strong advocates for years in the field of special education and early childhood, we find this to be one of the deterrents to children receiving quality instruction. Do not be afraid of discussing this topic openly with your leadership group. In fact, you will not be able to move forward with your goals if you do not agree on how children learn and what is important to teach. Record your research-based agreements and move forward.

When building a leadership group that will continue to work on your PreK–3 system, ensure that every member of your group has a sense of purpose and knows where you are going. In *The Way of the Shepherd: 7 Ancient Secrets to Managing Productive People*, Kevin Leman and William Pentak (2004) talk about how effective organizations and leaders infuse every position with importance. All group members share equal power and respect because of the important work they do, not because of their title or degree. This group will continue to grow as other preschools and providers learn about the work that you are doing. Welcome new members along the way; assign new members to an experienced member of your team to review the topics and research your group has gathered and your recorded agreements.

Guided by current research and armed with best-practice information, your leadership group will increase its ability to problem-solve and plan for the instructional needs of both the children and the teachers on the front lines in their programs or classrooms. In *12 Brain/ Mind Learning Principles in Action* (Caine, Caine, McClintic, & Klimek, 2009), the authors provide helpful guidance on instruction using brain research. They remind us that "the optimal emotional climate for learning is relaxed alertness," described as: "Even though I am challenged and excited (even anxious), I feel capable and trust in my abilities." A few of the researchers providing information on high-quality literacy instruction that makes a difference for children are Joe Torgesen, Jack Fletcher, and Sharon Vaughn. Their work on the effectiveness of targeted instruction that addresses the specific needs of children has been extremely helpful in building PreK–3 systems of support. Share this information with your leadership group when discussing quality early childhood instruction. We know it requires knowledgeable professionals to set up the optimal learning environment *and* teach the skills necessary with extensions and multiple practice opportunities that many children require to learn. To underscore the need for intentional instruction using brain-friendly strategies, we call this *multiple joyful practice opportunities*. We have found that instead of debating the issue of what not to teach, we should ask the question, "How can we teach these important skills in a fun and motivating way that leads to better outcomes for our children (more children experiencing the gift of reading)?"

Vision Plus Action

Your leadership group will want to continue to examine the research and collect data on how your children are doing on your established goals. In your leadership group, promote an environment of inquiry and celebration, confirm effective teaching and learning strategies, and learn numerous ways to reach more children.

In order to do this, follow these steps:

- Examine the research together and establish a common language centered around teaching and learning.
- Build on your strengths and inventory what you are already doing that is effective.
- Learn the most effective strategies from neuroscience to provide all children with the quality instruction and learning environment they require to reach their full potential.
- Formulate and implement a plan to provide all teaching staff with this critical information (monthly professional development).
- Establish core curriculum and supplemental materials.

- Agree on what assessment information you will gather to celebrate your success and revise instruction to reach more children.
- Formulate and implement a plan to provide families with this information.
- Establish broad-based support.
- Be strategic in your planning to finance your goals and publicize your success.
- Repeat the same steps for the next goal.

Establish a Common Language Centered Around Teaching and Learning

A unified PreK–3 approach requires a common language and agreement regarding the needs of children: What is important for children to learn during the PreK–3 years and why? What is the best way to teach young children? and How do we measure our efforts? Share new information and research that has direct implications for classroom instruction. Rather than debating the value of existing practices, apply current brain-based instructional methods to provide your children with the highest probability of success. Learning together as a community creates a synergy that fuels your efforts.

Moderate Cost Strategies

Bremerton School District in Bremerton, Washington, is an example of a high-poverty school district that has prioritized its resources to build a professional PreK–12 learning community. The district, under the leadership of Linda Jenkins, Assistant Superintendent and Curriculum Director, provided teachers and administrative staff with the background research knowledge to provide quality reading instruction for students. For example, Jack M. Fletcher, PhD, spoke to the entire community on learning disabilities. He defined characteristics of at-risk children, ways to intervene early, and most importantly, how to prevent academic casualties. This started a frenzy of excitement and hope. The fact that we could actually prevent learning disabilities became a unifying theme. Preschool providers took great pride in the fact that they could make a significant difference for children prior to entering kindergarten, and the K–12 staff learned the positive impact of focused core instruction and aligned interventions. To read more about learning disabilities, please see the recommended books and articles that unite your efforts in Resource A, beginning on page 140.

Gather the best researchers and invite them to your community when possible. Open up the discussion to families as well as teaching staff. This is another form of what we call "friendly accountability," when we all see and hear the same information and form an agreement as to what we will do with the information. For example, when parents heard how important it was to use research-based reading instruction, they were very interested in what type of reading curriculum and interventions we used and were supportive of spending funds for a reading adoption.

When families in your own community hear current research and realize the difference that early intervention and quality instruction makes for their children, they will seek out preschool and school district programs and services (PreK–3) that provide this.

In our community, we followed up with the following individuals:

- Dr. Louisa Moats spoke to our families and the PreK–12 teaching staff about the importance of vocabulary.
- Dan Reschly, PhD, Vanderbilt University, talked to our groups about learning disabilities and Response to Intervention (RTI).
- Kitsap Community Resources Head Start used their professional-development funds to bring in trainers in the area of early literacy and in the social and emotional domain.
- Dr. Jan Hasbrouck worked with our district on designing Tier I, II, and III reading instruction.
- Dr. Sharon Vaughn came to our community and spoke to staff and families.

These individuals were so gracious and were willing to help us to provide excellent instruction for children.

Look around; is there a respected researcher in the area of reading who may be speaking at a national or regional conference nearby? Send some of your leadership group to the conference and have them report back to the group. Many national conferences include scholarships for parents who represent an organization. Head Start, Title I, and Special Education are all possible funding sources that require that dollars be spent for specific professional development tied to student achievement. One of the international researchers who arrived in Bremerton to speak to our community sincerely asked the question, "I speak all over the world and in front of huge audiences; why am I in Bremerton of all places?" One author replied, "Because our children deserve the best and that is you. Thank you for coming."

Low- and No-Cost Strategies

You may be asking, "What if I cannot secure the funds to bring in this level of quality speakers to our community?" Do not settle for just anyone. It would be better to participate in book studies or literature circles. The following are low- to no-cost early reading resources:

- Examine your state's Early Learning and Development Benchmarks. Each state is required to develop standards or developmental benchmarks regarding what every child needs to know and be able to do prior to kindergarten. These and other state resources are available free online.
- Resource A lists recommended books, as well as free publications available from the U.S. government online.

It is also important for your group to examine books and current research regarding the prevention of learning disabilities. Check the following resources:

- The Center for the Improvement of Early Reading Achievement (CIERA) is a national center for research on early reading.
- The Learning Disabilities Association of America (LDA) has lots of free information to download.

Continue to engage your leadership group in discussions by asking questions such as: Why is this skill important to learn prior to kindergarten? What if we do not teach this? How do we appropriately teach this to young children? and How do we know we are reaching each child? Your group will want to divide the work of gathering information and bringing it back to the next several meetings; this will establish a common understanding and vocabulary for teaching and learning. Avoid the pitfall of processing too long; you will lose your group. Obtain a balance of chart paper discussion (used for brainstorming and processing activities) and recorded decision making.

Why Are Early Reading Skills (or Whatever Skill You're Working on) Important to Learn Prior to Kindergarten, And What Are the Implications For Children If We Do Not Teach Early Reading Skills?

Here are a few key questions and facts that we have found helpful when working to answer the question above and keep your group moving forward.

- The number of children with learning disabilities continues to increase. "Of those with 'specific learning disabilities,' 80 percent are there simply because they haven't learned how to read. Thus, many children receiving special education—up to 40 percent—are there because they weren't taught to read" (Ed Pubs, 2002)

- Difficulties in the areas of early language development, vocabulary, and phonological awareness are significant predictors of reading problems (Olofsson & Niedersoe, 1999; Glascoe & Robertshaw, 2007).

- The Matthew effect, the idea that the rich get richer and the poor get poorer, can be applied to vocabulary development (Stanovich, 1986). Emphasize the difference that PreK–3 staff can make in all areas of development when children expand their vocabulary and background knowledge. Children who are read to for less than one minute per day are exposed to 8,000 words per year versus 1,800,000 words when they are read to for 20 minutes per day.

- The Washington Research Institute and the University of Washington have developed a DVD series called *Language is the Key*, featuring dialogic reading strategies to build vocabulary. Available in multiple languages, the series provides teachers and parents with a specific CAR (Comment and wait, Ask questions and wait, and Respond by adding a little more) strategy designed to build vocabulary while reading.

What Do We Teach? Early Reading Is the Job of Early Childhood.

- Daily phonological awareness (The ability to manipulate sounds is highly correlated with reading success [Lundberg, Frost, & Petersen, 1988].)
- Listening, rhyming, sentence segmenting, syllable segmenting
- Rhyming (identifying and making oral rhymes at age three)
- Identifying and working with syllables in spoken words at age four
- Identifying and categorizing the first phoneme of words (your name!) with five-year-olds
- Alliteration (four- and five-year-olds)
- Letter-sound correspondence (four- and five-year-olds)
- Blending and segmentation (five-year-olds and above)

How Do We Teach?

- *Developing Early Literacy: Report of the National Early Literacy Panel* (National Institute for Literacy, 2008) describes the most effective research-based teaching strategies for early literacy.

- *Foundations for Success: The Final Report of the National Mathematics Advisory Panel* (2008) includes research-based instructional techniques for preschool.
- Successful teachers employ multiple joyful practice opportunities.

The Next Four Steps

1. Build on your strengths and inventory what you are already doing to build a strong early literacy foundation.

2. Learn the most effective teaching strategies that will provide all children with quality instruction and the learning environment they require to reach their full potential.

3. Formulate and implement a plan to provide all teaching staff with this critical information (monthly professional development).

4. Gather information to measure your results, self-reflect, and revise instruction.

An Example of Application

In our community, we shared the importance of rhyming for building an early reading skills foundation with our leadership group and community preschool teachers. The response was positive and had an immediate impact on a large number of children. We asked preschool teachers to inventory what they were already doing to teach rhyming: finger plays, books that rhyme, and songs and poems throughout the year and "sprinkled" throughout the day. The teachers gathered data on children who were already able to recognize and make a rhyme. Next, the leadership group planned monthly professional development. The teachers learned the importance of rhyming within the context of phonological awareness and exchanged intentional teaching strategies and created materials to provide more focused instruction and practice opportunities throughout the day aligned to what the children were learning in the classroom. In a short amount of time, these same teachers returned to the monthly preschool teacher's professional development to celebrate and record their success on significantly increasing the number of children in each class who were able to rhyme and participate in rhyming activities.

Following any successful effort, have your leadership group publicize your results, and ask your community for additional support. For example, call your local paper, advertise on your school Web site and reader board, and elicit the help of your local library, pediatricians, newspapers, community Web sites, and clubs to get quality rhyming books, poetry, and music into the hands of your children and families.

Provide Teachers With the Tools They Need to Reach Your Goals

Across our nation, the early childhood preschool classrooms and programs are as diverse in their curriculum implementation as the K–3 public school system. For years, we struggled in the area of preschool special education to modify and adjust curriculum for children with disabilities served in inclusive preschool settings. We know who when we start with a consistent curriculum and classroom routines and procedures, it makes it so much easier to adapt to children who have disabilities or help children who are struggling. A consistent community-selected curriculum that matches your established goal(s), combined with monthly professional development and aligned to your K–3 standards, is the optimum. Bremerton School District and their Early Childhood Care and Education group (community preschools) selected an early reading curriculum that all the ECCE community preschool partners use. The school district purchases the curriculum and loans it to their preschool partners. Other school districts have followed their lead. At the time of publication, one classroom set of the preschool early reading curriculum costs $2,000. We calculated that every child who enters kindergarten without the necessary early reading foundational skills, and as a result requires remediation, costs $2,500 *per year* from kindergarten through twelfth grade. All it takes is *one* child to enter kindergarten with solid foundational skills from *one* partner preschool that uses that curriculum to recover your initial cost. Other potential funding sources are discussed in Step 9. If you are not able to secure funding for curriculum at this point, continue with the activities mentioned above and look at low-cost options. However, know that a research-based curriculum selected and used by all your community preschool partners will accelerate your timeline and ability to reach more children.

Minimum Cost for Curriculum Selection

Roger Long, PhD, Whitworth College, and Marcy Stein, PhD, University of Washington, Tacoma, developed a curriculum selection process that has been extremely helpful in our work building PreK–3 systems. Roger facilitated our community preschool curriculum selection. His skills fostered an environment of inquiry and respectful communication with a constant focus on the children. He has worked with our community and others. We have adapted this same process and shared it with a variety of communities and school districts. The most important part of this process is to ensure that your community chooses the curriculum based on research aligned with your state's early learning and K–3 standards. This does not work as well if the school district or state selects the curriculum and dictates to the preschools what to use. Because fidelity of implementation is so critical to success, you want to ensure that this curriculum is worthy of the effort.

You might consider implementing the following procedure:

1. Arrange for or hire an outside facilitator. If you do not have the funds, trade with someone. You do a presentation on early childhood development for them, and they facilitate this process for you. You need a person who is able to encourage discussion and keep the group focused on the topic. This allows you to provide input and participate in the process.

2. Call all early childhood curriculum publishers and tell them you are going through an adoption process. Ask them to send you any curriculum on early reading that they would like you to consider. Let them know that publishers should not contact your committee; if they do, their materials will not be considered. While materials are arriving, keep this process moving.

3. Have representation on your community curriculum committee from all your partner preschools. Include preschool teachers and directors.

4. At your initial meeting, invite representatives that can speak to the variety of considerations you will need to address when seeking a research-based (validated if possible) curriculum. Among others, this list may include the following:

- Head Start guidelines
- Faith-based preschools
- Special education regulations
- Your state's Early Learning and Development Benchmarks
- K–3 state standard alignment
- Ideally, you should also find someone to address what is essential to teach at the preschool level in your goal area (early reading). There are several curriculum choices that can be used in conjunction with the mandated programs that are used by Head Start and faith-based preschools.

5. At the next meeting, establish a rubric of what you need in an early childhood curriculum to meet the needs of the children you

serve and address your established goal(s). For example, you might want to emphasize a strong vocabulary and an oral-language component that is explicitly taught. We encourage you to include cost, ease of implementation, and assessment in your rubric. See the curriculum adoption form in Resource D for one example.

6. At the following meeting, put all the early childhood materials that you have gathered out on tables and divide your participants into groups of four. The groups should rotate to each table, using the rubric your community developed to evaluate and score curriculum and select your top three.

7. The next time you meet, invite the publishers or representatives of your top three to present their curriculum. All participants will use their notes and established rubric to ask questions to make their final selection. When possible, negotiate the cost of materials, professional development, and coaching for at least the first and second year of implementation. You want to make sure that you see the positive results of your investment the very first year. You do not want one child to miss the benefit of quality instruction.

Low- to No-Cost Curriculum Options

In the absence of a community-selected research-based early learning curriculum, you will need to spend more time on establishing the common language and structure by doing the following:

1. Conduct a review of current research and best practices. Select the highest level of validity (meta-analysis when possible).

2. Review state Early Learning and Development Benchmarks and program standards.

3. Conduct a strength–based inventory of what every preschool is already doing.

4. Create core materials, activities, and instructional practices aligned to the early learning benchmarks and your goals.

5. Create or purchase supplemental materials to provide additional teaching and learning opportunities aligned to your selected goals (increasing early reading skills).

6. Establish consistent routines and instructional procedures.

7. Gather data to review and refine your instruction.

When working with your leadership group to design curriculum materials and outline research-based instructional practices, be sure to record your work along the way. We have found it helpful to ask the group to commit to documenting what is working (quality instruction) for children so that all can modify or replicate the efforts. This will allow your team to move forward, celebrate, and publicize what is working so your organization can continue to expand and improve your instruction.

Quality Preschool

One of the many ongoing topics of discussion at your leadership group as you develop a common language will be your definition of a *quality preschool*. What does quality look like in your community? What will be your standard of excellence and commitment to the families that choose your preschool? These questions go far beyond early reading and are ones that your leadership group needs to address. The following sources may be helpful for your discussions regarding what quality looks like in your community:

- "From Rhetoric to Reality: The Case for Compensation for Prekindergarten Education" (Neuman, 2003)
- *Nurturing Knowledge: Building a Foundation for School Success by Linking Early Literacy to Math, Science, Art, and Social Studies* (Neuman, Roskos, Wright, & Lenhart, 2007)
- "Changing the Odds" (Neuman, 2007)

Try reading the article "From Rhetoric to Reality" using a jigsaw method with your leadership group and preschool teachers. Divide into four groups to read about and define what "high-quality compensatory (prekindergarten) programs should include: sufficient time, precise targeting, thoughtful focus, and accountability for results." Under each of the four components, list characteristics that you'd like to see if you walked into one of your community partner preschool classrooms. (See Figure 3.1.) Have the group members agree on four descriptors under each category that would describe the highest-quality preschool, one suitable for their own child's participation. Record your agreements and create a two-page document with your leadership group's name on the top.

Use this document for walk-throughs to share with classroom visitors and families. Walk- throughs are also known as *learning walks* or *instructional rounds*. This form of professional development includes teachers and administrators setting personal goals and observing classrooms. This is another part of what we call our "friendly accountability system." This important component to creating a PreK–3 system continues to move your efforts forward and responds to the needs of your community.

| Figure 3.1 | Look Fors in Early Childhood Centers of Excellence Walk-Throughs |

Sufficient Time *(for learning)*	**Thoughtful Focus on Learning** *Powerful learning opportunities/activities planned by experienced team of professionals*
1. 2. 3. 4.	1. 2. 3. 4.
Precise Targeting *Services and supports targeted for children who are struggling and children who need to be challenged*	**Accountability** *Professionals know what each child's abilities and needs are using multiple classroom observations and assessment. This information is used to assist and guide each child to the next level.*
1. 2. 3. 4.	1. 2. 3. 4.
Comments:	

Another simple way of confirming your group's commitment to quality is by creating a "Best Places" logo for your community partners. Bremerton School District and their community preschools created a window display illustrated in Figure 3.2. Bremerton community preschools display their Early Childhood Care and Education (ECCE) logo with pride. Many families in that community look for the logo when selecting a quality preschool. In order for community preschools to display it in their window, they must commit to the following:

1. A school district and community preschool partnership

2. Using the community-selected preschool curriculum

3. The preschool director, coordinator, or head teacher participating in the leadership group

4. The teaching staff participating in monthly professional development

5. Participating in the "assessment loop," a respectful review of data on the children they sent to kindergarten

6. Celebrating and adjusting their programs and instruction

Figure 3.2

Early Childhood Care & Education

Bremerton School District

A Community
Working Together
Wonders of Learning Preschool
AND
Bremerton School District
Building Early Literacy Skills

Wonders of Learning Preschool

Gather Assessment Information and Revise Instruction

Your leadership group will decide how to measure the success of your efforts and the growth made by your children. In Step 1, we talked about the use of assessment to gather local data on children entering kindergarten to establish your community needs. We will talk more about what we call the *assessment loop* and *friendly accountability* in Step 5. Ask your leadership group to examine its goals and determine what measurements you will use to gauge its progress.

For the first question, How are your preschool partners progressing toward your established goal? it is important that you foster a climate of inquiry, with respectful examination of kindergarten entrance data that puts the needs of children at the center of the conversation. Using Step 1, you have already gathered baseline data from the previous year on your PreK–3 or K–3 children. If your community's data are consistent with the national average, your data looks bleak. Nationwide, children continue to enter our schools behind and thus remain behind. Now you will be able to approach your fall data with anticipation of better results. We suggest sending home a letter from the school district to all the families of your preschool partners letting them know that you and the community preschool are working together to provide children with the necessary skills they need to have a firm foundation prior to kindergarten. As part of your efforts this year, evaluate all kindergarten children at the end of September to find out what they already know and are able to do in the area of early reading. Give this information back to their preschool teacher so that you and the preschool can celebrate the success and growth the children have made and adjust their program to reach even more children. Share with parents the information on the assessment instrument you are using and give them an opportunity to opt out if necessary. We have found that parents find the information most helpful. Preschools have gained more respect and popularity from families for their partnership with the school district and their willingness to look at their own practices and improve. Have kindergarten teachers share with preschool teachers how they use these assessment tools to adjust their instruction, not to label children or to advise parents to keep their children home another year. Concentrate on the assessments that align with your first year's goals. You may decide that your current assessments used at kindergarten in the fall are not beneficial for program adjustment, and you may need to choose another measure. At the preschool level, an examination of the use of screening tools may be helpful. When our leadership group made a careful examination of the screening instruments used, we found duplication, and, in many cases, the information was not used to adjust programming for children.

For discussion on the second question, How do you know that the children you have this year are getting the instruction and learning opportunities they need while they are still in your care? you may need to build your preschool assessment bank to include formal and informal assessments based on the initial domain(s) you selected. For example, if you want children to have the early reading foundational skills they need and that are appropriate to teach prior to kindergarten, you will need to select key early reading skills to take a "dip stick" measurement. The goal here is to determine if children need additional practice opportunities and more intentional teaching using the best practices and research-based strategies.

Teach these skills in fun and motivating ways that are infused throughout the day and make them part of your intentional instructional plan. Be cautious of creating disjointed instruction by randomly sprinkling isolated tasks into your classroom. This only adds to the difficulties that many children experience when trying to focus their attention on the lesson.

How to Engage Parents and Exchange Information

One of your leadership group's many tasks is to formulate a plan on how to provide families with the same valuable information that you are learning regarding children's development and teaching and learning. It was a humbling experience when we realized that preschool parents are not especially interested in what the school district has to say. Parents want to know what their child's preschool teacher has to say. It is all about relationships and trust. Now we have far greater success at engaging parents and exchanging information to help their children through our preschool partners. When preschool teachers talk positively about their child's future school or kindergarten teacher, it builds a positive school-family relationship. When kindergarten teachers and principals know that their community preschool providers honor and build on the work being done prior to kindergarten, children do not have to lose valuable time, and parents receive consistent, accurate information. Include how to get the word out to parents in your monthly professional development trainings. Your teachers are very skilled at reaching parents. Information on exchanging a variety of activities and materials that support your parents will be included in Step 4.

STEP 3 AT A GLANCE

- Examine the research in your leadership group together and establish a common language around teaching and learning.
- Build on your strengths, and inventory what you are already doing that is effective.
- Strive for excellence by learning the most effective instructional strategies that provide all children with the quality learning environment they require to reach their full potential.
- Formulate and implement a plan to provide all teaching staff with this critical information (monthly professional development).
- Establish a core curriculum, supplemental materials, and a common language.
- Define *quality*.
- Agree on what assessment information you will gather to celebrate your success and to revise instruction to reach more children.
- Formulate and implement a plan to engage families and exchange ideas.
- Repeat the same steps for the next domain (goal area) you choose to work on as a group.

Next Step: Provide high-quality professional development and the tools teachers want and need to do this work.

Step 4

High-Quality Professional Development

Never doubt that a small group of thoughtful, committed citizens can change the world. Indeed it is the only thing that ever has.

–Margaret Mead

Congratulations! You are the ones who will change the educational lives of the children in your community forever! You are well on your way to making a difference. Now it is time to build a strong professional-development component to support your PreK–3 system. Duane Baker, from the Baker Evaluation Research & Consulting Group, stated, "The closer you are to the classroom, the greater the impact you have." As early childhood classroom teachers and providers, you have the potential to make a significant difference in the lives of the children in your community. If the overall goal is to have children enter kindergarten ready to learn, we must develop an intentional, professional staff development plan to ensure that those who are closest to the children have the resources and information needed to maximize their efforts.

How to Provide Professional Development Aligned to Your Goals

This important work requires that everyone on your team has a firm grasp of the research and components of the best instructional practices. The 2009 National Association for the Education of Young Children (NAEYC) position statement indicates that there are many teachers who "lack current knowledge and skills needed to provide high-quality care and education to young children." An important part of professional development is the ability to present information in a real and relevant manner so that your teachers have the skills and knowledge necessary to provide a high-quality experience for all children in their care. Step 4 consists of the following two parts:

1. Gathering information for a strong foundation for teachers

2. Establishing your professional development system

Gathering Information for a Strong Foundation for Teachers

The first part involves gathering information in order to strengthen the background knowledge of all your community preschool partners. Based on the goals set by your leadership group, begin by gathering current information and research to support your efforts. The group can decide the parameters for the type of works to include, and then each member can be responsible for collecting these documents.

One of the topics you will want to address upfront involves developmentally appropriate practices, assessment concerns, and any other current issues. In the early childhood field, there is concern about maintaining developmentally appropriate practices. Providing accurate research based on the appropriate methods to teach young children will help clarify this important issue. Here are some resources to study as a group to provide a strong foundation for your members:

- The report *Developmentally Appropriate Practice in Early Childhood Programs Serving Children From Birth Through Age 8* (NAEYC, 2009) provides relevant information from the National Association for the Education of Young Children, an organization responsible for defining the best practices in the field of early childhood. This report provides five critical components of developmentally appropriate practices, including assessment.

- *Where We Stand: On Curriculum, Assessment, and Program Evaluation* (NAEYC, 2004) will assist you in clarifying issues.
- The book *Nurturing Knowledge: Building a Foundation for School Success by Linking Early Literacy to Math, Science, Art, and Social Studies* (Neuman, Roskos, Wright, & Lenhart, 2007) provides research and practical applications for classrooms.

Prepare the adult learning environment by building a high-quality professional development system that provides teachers with the current research in a friendly, nonthreatening environment, paired with practical applications. The Minnesota Early Literacy Training Project (MELT) determined that practical, fun, hands-on activities were the biggest needs of teachers. They also wanted "site specific" support to increase their ability to help children develop early literacy skills (Craig-Unkefer, McConnell, Morgan, & Schwabe, 2005). Acknowledge that teachers want to increase their knowledge in effective teaching and learning practices to create high-quality classroom environments that will maximize the learning of their children. When teachers have the information to make important changes and understand the rationale behind what they are doing, they are able to create wonderful opportunities to benefit children.

While forming your professional development system, be sure to include important information on developing self-efficacy skills for the teachers as well as the children. It is essential to retain development of social and emotional skills that have been a cornerstone of early childhood, while increasing your literacy focus. By connecting research to the teacher's own learning environments, the trainings become useful and have direct impact on the children and their families.

Early childhood professionals are very passionate about their responsibilities to children in their care. Your job is to gather the evidence, based on the benefit to children, to unite your group to ensure the success of each child. In their book, *Ready or Not*, Valora Washington and Stacie Goffin discuss the impact this has on the growth and recognition of the field (Goffin & Washington, 2007). The early childhood profession does not even use a consistent name; this lack of unity and cohesiveness can be detrimental to our children and our goal to ensure the success of each child. Our children deserve the best-prepared teachers and the latest information. For the first time in history, the focus is on early childhood resources, policy, and legislation. We know that this stage in children's lives (birth–age 8) is the time of greatest brain development; growth is rapid, and the brain is the most malleable. It is our job as professionals to learn about and understand the research and apply it to our current practices. For example, in the area of reading, experts agree that early intervention is the best way to prevent reading difficulties, yet there are some who still operate as though reading develops similar to language. What will you do if the research does not follow your beliefs about young children?

Here are some additional facts that we found useful to guide our professional development:

- Children who have not developed some basic literacy skills by the time they enter school are three to four times more likely to drop out in later years (*National Adult Literacy Survey*, 2002).

- In 1999, only 53 percent of children ages three to five were read to daily by a family member. Children in families with incomes below the poverty line are less likely to be read to aloud everyday than are children in families with incomes at or above the poverty line (*The Condition of Education 2006: Fast Facts Family Reading*, National Center for Education Statistics, 2006).

- Instruction appears to establish the neural networks that support reading. No child is born a reader; all children in literate societies must be taught how to read.

- Early intervention can greatly reduce the number of older children who are identified as learning disabled (LD). Without early identification, children typically require intensive, long-term special education programs, which have meager results. Early intervention allows ineffective remedial programs to be replaced with effective prevention, while providing older students who continue to need services with enhanced instruction so they can return to the educational mainstream (Lyon & Fletcher, 2001).

Target Professional Development to the Needs of Your Community

The professional development of teachers is related to the quality of early childhood programs, and program quality predicts developmental outcomes for children. Formal early childhood education and training have been linked consistently to positive caregiver behaviors. The strongest relationship is found between the number of years of education and training and the appropriateness of a teacher's classroom behavior (Bowman, Donnovan, & Burns, 2000).

Determine what your teaching staff requires to do this important work. For the purposes of this book, the goals are literacy based, with the goal of increasing the number of children entering kindergarten with early literacy skills. If your group selects other goals, the process outlined in building a strong professional development component is the same. The goals that the leadership group established for the children in your community will guide your trainings. They are the pathway to success for your children. Be sure to infuse the importance of providing brain-based instruction to how young children learn throughout the trainings. Teachers and staff need to be aware that by focusing on literacy you are not ignoring social and emotional skills. Research is clear that information cannot be processed and available for higher-thinking skills without going through the limbic system, Figure 4.1. This system is responsible for the input of information

Figure 4.1 Brain

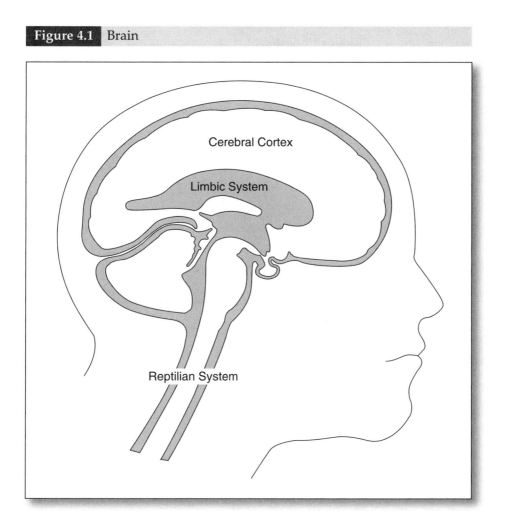

and the retrieval of long-term memory (Willis, 2007). Barbara Bowman and her colleagues also describe the importance of focusing on all areas of development for our preschool-aged children:

> Cognitive, social-emotional, and motor development are complementary, mutually supportive areas of growth all requiring active attention in the preschool years. Social skills and physical dexterity influence cognitive development, just as cognition plays a role in children's social understanding and motor competence. All are therefore related to early learning and later academic achievement and are necessary domains of early childhood pedagogy (Bowman, Donnovan, & Burns, 2000).

Meet the Needs of a Wide Variety of Learners

Flexibility in implementation of the trainings and alignment to district and state standards are keys to creating a professional learning community; early childhood programs are as diverse as their staff's development needs. If your partnership includes community preschools, faith-based programs, and center-based and in-home child care professionals, there will be a wide range of learners. Some will have high school diplomas, GEDs, or their CDA (Child Development Associates); others may have two-year associate's, bachelor's, or master's degrees. In any given community, early childhood environments vary from large center-based facilities to in-home providers where one person is solely responsible for all aspects of the program, or from faith-based preschools to school district programs. Some teachers will be able to attend group trainings, others will not. Let your belief that each person has valuable input and deserves equal access to this process be your guiding principle. Your professional learning community needs to be able to accommodate all members. Therefore, to reach all members, your system needs to be multitiered and able to provide learning and benefit to all staff needs. How will you ensure that all members have the information they need to succeed? In addition to the uniqueness of in-home providers, what other considerations does your community present? Is your community small, with only one or two child care centers? Is there currently an informal group already established that could become the professional learning community to undertake your established goals or help to spread the word about your trainings? What are some cultural considerations? This is one of those opportunities for brainstorming solutions. At your meeting, in the middle of the table, either literally or figuratively, children should be in the center and at the heart of your conversations. Set child-focused goals to remind everybody that the child is the center of the discussion.

Establishing Your Professional Development System

Help your group select common days and times that are available to most teachers for your monthly trainings. Are there currently consistent days that most programs meet? If not, is it possible to change that, so that most teachers and providers could attend your training? Because your group created goals for children and fostered a culture of inquiry, you are able to creatively problem-solve to address each program's professional development needs and other issues as they arise.

The length of time for your trainings could vary depending on your group. If the trainings are too brief, it will be difficult to provide in-depth information or engage in discussion. If they are longer than three hours, it is difficult for centers to release teachers for the training, and teachers become anxious to return to their classes or other duties. Trainings that last about three hours can include review of the information presented the previous month, and teachers can show examples of how they implemented the information in their classes from what they learned the previous month. Discussion, which focuses on the variety of activities completed, serves to deepen the understanding as well as provide even more examples of hands-on application of the information. Teachers are great at "piggybacking" on each other's ideas and activities, and often, this discussion leads to even more in-depth knowledge and applications.

Determine your monthly training location. It can be enlightening for teachers to rotate the training among the community preschool partners. By visiting other sites, providers can experience additional learning environments, gain new ideas, and often get re-energized about their own classrooms. For the hosting provider, it grants the chance to display the results of hard work and demonstrate pride in the implementation of past training topics. It also builds the excitement, such as what happens when "company is coming," and provides an opportunity for self-reflection. While preparing their room for the "company," teachers can ask questions that can guide their preparation and self-reflection. Have I created a quality-learning environment? Have I incorporated the research into my own classroom? Is it making a positive impact for children and their families? Encouraging preschool teachers to host the training is an effective friendly accountability strategy.

During the training, honor the adult learner; start on time, provide breaks, and offer wonderful snacks. Since preschool teachers are on the floor with children all day, have comfortable adult chairs whenever possible; one adult remarked, "on Friday, I deserve to sit in a big chair!"

Training Format

The format for the monthly professional trainings may need modification or adjustment over time. Use a consistent format, so that adults can focus their attention on the important aspects. Components of each monthly professional development consist of the following:

- A half hour to welcome, review, share, and celebrate success
- A quarter to one-half hour to connect your current topic to your foundation
- A half to three-quarters of an hour of new information
- Three-quarters to one hour for practical application
- Three-quarters to one hour to complete "make and take" activity (more on this later in this chapter) to use on Monday morning

Review and Celebrate Small Successes

At the beginning of the training, develop an exercise to review the information from the last month. It could be a game, activity, or discussion. Also take a few minutes to invite teachers to share successes from the past month; it could be anecdotal information, pictures, or work samples. Highlight programs for implementing research or activities from the last training that had a positive impact on children. If any program received awards or newspaper coverage, recognize it also.

Connect Your Current Topic to Your Foundation

After recognizing implementation and successes since the last training, provide information to connect your current topic to one of the foundational pieces set by your leadership group. By intentionally discussing how the current topic fits into the overall plan and other professional development, you will be supporting the entire system. The trainings will not appear to be random topics without any basis or thought to their use and selection. This connection of new information to prior knowledge is consistent with brain-based learning.

Provide Research and New Information

Next, the trainer presents new information based on topics previously determined by the leadership group; this could be new research or vital changes published, such as information from the National Early Literacy Panel or National Math Panel, or topics based on data. Depending on the group, it could be essentials such as foundational knowledge that everybody needs to understand, or it could build on the group's common knowledge. The level of sophistication in teacher conversations is elevated and focused on children when teachers become well versed in research and take pride in its implementation. This high expectation and sophisticated knowledge sets the tone for new members. Partners attending conferences or other trainings report that they "already knew the information" and were surprised when others did not. It becomes readily apparent that this is not the norm everywhere. Some examples of topics include the following:

- Phonological awareness (listening, rhyming, segmenting, blending)
- Oral language and vocabulary
- Alphabetic principle and print awareness
- Teaching letter names and sounds
- Importance of background knowledge for later comprehension
- Useful assessment data
- Preschool curriculum training

Practical Application: Classroom

Teachers are interested in practical, hands-on application of new knowledge or research, especially how to apply it to their own learning environment. When information is useful and readily available to use in their classroom, it increases the probability of its implementation. One core principle of the training is to share information, skills, and activities that can literally be used on Monday morning to benefit children and families.

Save your teachers hours of prep time by providing activities and materials they can easily put together and use. Tangible, practical examples increase the likelihood of implementing the information. Here are a few:

- Teachers, who have already applied the information or the materials, can provide examples. This keeps the discussion real and relevant. It also increases ownership of the information; teachers often comment, "I do that" or "I want to try that."
- Share classroom videos, photos, and other developed activities that demonstrate the application of the research. Teachers take pride in sharing their successes. If you have a coach, that person can facilitate obtaining this media; it is critical to honor teachers, yet not to create extra work for them.
- Table discussions can be structured to facilitate more opportunities for participation rather than just whole-group discussion.

- With a "think/pair/share" exercise, time is provided for each person to think about the topic under discussion. Partners then discuss it with each other before sharing their discussion with the rest of the table. One representative from each table then synthesizes the information and shares it with the entire group.
- Jigsaws are an effective method to disseminate and discuss written information. The entire group is numbered according to the number of topics to be discussed. Participants with the same number meet and read, discuss, and become "experts" on the information assigned to them. Then they go back to their original table and teach the information to the rest of the table group. At the end of the given time, everybody at the table has learned all of the information. The information can then be discussed as a whole group if feasible or desired.
- Gallery walks allow participants an opportunity to move around the room. Charts are placed around the room with a topic, subtopic, or question written on the top of each one. The participants answer the question or brainstorm ideas to go with the topic and write them on the paper. The facilitator determines when the groups move to the next chart; the new group adds new ideas or indicates agreement or disagreement with ideas already on the chart. After all groups have rotated to all charts, a group discussion takes place.

Family Engagement: The Home Environment

After the teachers have heard the research and its application for their classroom, the next step is to encourage families with this information. This will extend the children's learning environment and expand opportunities for their growth. As part of each training plan, provide time for teachers to translate the information into parent-friendly terms to support children in their home environments. Parents trust and value their child's teacher. They are more willing to hear ways to support their child for school success from their own teachers than by attending training presented by the school district staff. Ongoing information delivered by the teacher may be a more effective method for reaching families who lack time or are uncomfortable attending formal presentations. It also avoids the dangers of one-time presentations with limited possibility of change. This cycle of providing information to the community preschool teachers, who have an established relationship with families, who present it to the parents, who then incorporate it into their child's daily life, creates a continuous learning environment for children and enriches your system of support. Other strategies to connect with families include: creating a "family literacy corner" with activities that families and children can engage in during drop off and pick up, using materials from the make and take to send home in bags for additional multiple joyful practice opportunities, and subscribing to a newsletter such as *First Teacher* (Parenting Matters Foundation) for your families. Some programs have backpacks with books for children to take home and read; the books are rotated weekly.

Low-Cost Training Options

Focusing on research is an excellent starting point for your professional development. By devoting one month to each area of phonological awareness and the remainder of the school year to the other four areas in the "big five" ideas for reading (phonological awareness, alphabetic principle, vocabulary, comprehension, and fluency with text), your entire first year is planned. Contact others throughout your school district, local educational service district, or state department who are experts in your goal areas to provide training for your group. It is possible to enlist the services of these individuals at no cost to the school district. The following are some low- or no-cost training options:

- *Developing Early Literacy: Report of the National Early Literacy Panel* (National Institute for Literacy, 2008)

- *The Report of the National Reading Panel: Teaching Children to Read* (NICHD, The Eunice Kennedy Shriver National Institute of Child Health and Human Development, 2000)

- *Foundations for Success: The Final Report of the National Mathematics Advisory Panel* (U.S. Department of Education, 2008)

- Use of instructional coaches to train on the preschool curriculum

- Explore the use of a "trainer of trainer" model, where coaches attend trainings and then train other district and community teachers

Training considerations are more complex, but not impossible, if the group does not have a common curriculum. You can use the above resources to create your own training sequence or use the Early Learning and Development Benchmarks and the kindergarten elementary school standards for your state. Examine the benchmarks related to your goals to determine what your children should currently be doing; use the kindergarten state standards to see expectations once they leave preschool. Decide on the skills that need to be taught to meet these benchmarks and identify the gaps, if any, between preschool and kindergarten standards. This is more time and labor intensive than having a published curriculum, but it is sound instructional practice to align your curriculum with the standards.

Make and Take Activity

The make and take activity is a valuable component of your monthly professional development. It allows teachers to apply the information on Monday morning. We have all been to conferences or trainings and returned with lots of information and no time to apply it. Your make and take will be the bridge between the information just presented and classroom implementation. It could be something used daily in the classroom, an activity for small-group or free-choice time, a teacher-led activity, or something that parents receive. You provide the materials specific to the project and, ideally, a laminator to add durability to the children's papers; the teachers bring their own basic art supplies.

Celebrating Your Successes

To honor the hard work of the teachers, consider a formal process to recognize growth and celebrate successes. This helps to create a cohesive learning community. At the beginning of the training, and throughout the year, find reasons to celebrate your success. The following are some suggestions to do just that:

- Spotlight local media reports of positive events regarding early childhood or reports that highlight efforts of group members.

- When the group or individual members receive an award, invite the agency to re-present it at a training or leadership group meeting; let everybody share the good success.

- Acknowledge personal or classroom endeavors during the review portion of the trainings. Providing avenues for teacher's self-reflection also honors hard work and accomplishments.

- Provide an intentional method for teachers who are not able to attend trainings to share their successes with the group via reports or other visual means.

- Develop a PowerPoint slide show using video clips that demonstrate each class's proudest moments.

- Create a book with the teachers on a specific topic studied; teachers can submit digital photos and captions on numerous subtopics selected by the group. The book could illustrate each concept with concrete photos and captions that describe the activity and its importance; each learning environment can submit its own information, or an instructional coach could obtain it.

- Designing a book to share information with families would be an excellent way to honor a teacher's work as well as benefit families. Each month select a different subtopic around a central theme; teachers bring their ideas on the importance of the topic and activities that families can engage in to support it at home as well as during daily activities. For the books, compile the information into pages and add clip art or actual digital photos. Find a design editor or other skilled person to compile the information and make it attractive; make sure to proofread it for clarity for your intended audience. Your group may have a parent willing to undertake this project.

- Produce a DVD highlighting the teachers and their work.

These projects could also function as training materials for new members. Keep a master binder of the handouts and information presented each month. This creates an archive of the trainings and helps new members to have access to past topics. The end of the school year is an excellent time to publicize and share successes. These celebration projects seem to increase in size, scope, and fun each year.

Information to Refine Your Work and Strive for Excellence

An important principle to keep in mind is to continue to review, refine, and revisit your efforts. When we are teaching or planning for any other important work, we continually monitor progress. This endeavor is not any different; do not celebrate your successes for too long without considering ways to make them even stronger.

Assess the Gains

How will you know that your hard work and changes are providing the desired results? Decide on some method, formal or informal, to assess the progress quickly. In literacy, specific to phonological awareness, one measure is to evaluate children's ability to rhyme, since it is a beginning component of phonological awareness. By using a few well-chosen activities, the assessment activity can take place within the typical daily routine during small-group instruction or individual work time activities. Ask the teachers to bring current information on the skill you are assessing to your monthly meetings.

This serves to keep the focus on your goal. With intentional focus on one skill, results can be dramatic, and all can celebrate your results and the impact you are making for children. See Figure 4.2.

Figure 4.2   Intentional Focus on Rhyming

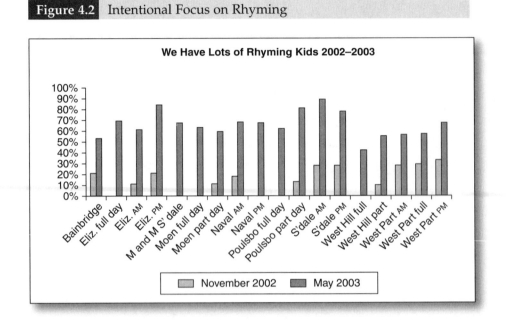

Use A Strength-Based Inventory to Find Out What Teachers Already do to Improve the Lives of Children.

The following are some suggestions your leadership group can offer on how to do this:

- Determine what activities or curriculum members of your group are already using regarding your goals.
- "Adopt an area": choose an area of the classroom and infuse reading throughout the area for the school year.
- Document (video, photos, or demonstration) your literacy-enhanced area: how are reading activities incorporated throughout the day in the classroom?
- Share the work from each classroom with the rest of the group to increase everyone's knowledge.

Raise Your Expectations

Each year refine your system and raise your expectations; do not be satisfied with the status quo. Look at your children's results: did you meet your goals? Loop your professional development to the PreK–3 system; include information from their trainings on brain research and other appropriate topics into your trainings. Scaffold new learning onto previous learning; new members will learn the past information, while current participants will increase the depth of their knowledge.

Keep a master copy of the photos and training materials as a reference for new members and a celebration of the journey. Each teacher keeps his or her own reference book; the handouts, activities, research, and notes are all in one location for future reference.

Refine Your Work (Friendly Accountability)

The saying "What you notice is what you get!" usually applies to situations regarding behavior. In this case, it refers to creating ways to keep your goals in sight without being punitive or overbearing. We refer to this as *friendly accountability*. The following are strategies to refine your work and keep your goals in sight:

- Discuss the importance of setting high expectations.
- Collect assessment information.
- Assess, and then use, information to benefit children and programs.
- Lead a discussion regarding the ramifications of the results and any action needed.
- The group decides when its children should master a particular skill.
- Rotate the training sites to different classrooms. (Company is coming!)

Use Job-Embedded Coaching and Follow-Through

Identify an individual who contacts members, coordinates the trainings, provides resources, and supports child care professionals. If your school district includes the use of instructional coaches, they are a valuable resource to assist you in your efforts. Many Head Start programs also have literacy specialists. Job-embedded professional development provides targeted learning opportunities for growth within the context of each teacher's learning environment. Coaches are able to provide assistance and resources targeted to each teacher's specific needs. Based on the research of Picus and associates, coaches have the greatest impact. The effect size of using coaches for professional development and training is 1.25 to 2.70 (effect sizes greater than 0.25 are significant, and those greater than 0.50 are substantial [Fermanich, Pincus, Odden, Mangan, Gross, & Rudo, 2006]). Use coaches who have established relationships with teachers and have classroom experience. Therefore, they are able to tailor information learned at the literacy trainings, make suggestions, and provide additional resources and materials to meet the needs of each unique learning environment.

In 2005, the University of Minnesota Early Literacy Training Project (MELT) researchers took their coaching model one-step further and created a "data-driven, relationship-based" coaching model. Their number one finding indicated that this model promotes teacher growth. Researchers Scott McConnell, Michael Rodriquez, and Paul van den Broek compared two professional development models of early childhood providers; one group received training only, and the other group received the same training as well as coaching that followed a set procedure. They conducted evaluations of both classrooms using an environmental rating scale known as the Early Language and Literacy Classroom Observation (ELLCO), and the children were assessed using the Individual Growth Development Indicators (IGDI), a comprehension measure; Concept About Print (CAP); and the Peabody Picture Vocabulary Test III (PPVT-III).

Using the ELLCO as the objective measure, the coaching group showed an increase of 38 percent compared to 16 percent on literacy activities (reading and writing) for the group who received training only. The coached group also showed an increase in "literacy-rich environments" of 57 percent, compared to 6 percent for the training-only group. Their conclusions:

> Overall, coaching appeared to solidify learning and provide for more consistency in how learning translated into practice. Improvements in physical environments and the increase in literacy activities practiced in the coaching centers directly reflected key areas emphasized in coaching. In contrast, the training-only centers early report showed relatively little growth in these areas and, in fact, experienced a decline in literacy activities over the course of the year following training (Lizakowski, T., "Minnesota Early Literacy Training Project," 2005).

The University of Kansas's Center for Research on Learning identified behavior, content knowledge, instruction, and formative assessment as the "big four" of essential framework components for coaches. Each coach is responsible for learning additional coaching strategies and techniques as well as for deepening his or her own knowledge of scientifically based reading research.

The Passport to Success program, sponsored by the Maryland State Department of Special Education, requires two weeks of training for new coaches. This includes theory, teaching strategies, and routines to share with teachers; each summer they attend another weeklong institute. Coaches need to be highly trained, flexible, and adept at establishing and maintaining relationships with teachers and directors.

As evidenced by the University of Minnesota MELT project, coaching alone is not enough to solidify and maintain gains or for training to translate into practice in the classroom. The coach is an important key to enabling busy teachers to be able to carry out this important work. Coaches can help teachers solve the logistical problems that might arise when implementing new practices. With the leadership group setting the training topics, and the teachers receiving the information and application strategies, a culture of learning is established. This creates a common language, which facilitates communication during meetings and trainings. This "top-down" and "bottom-up" model provides for greater likelihood of implementing the skills. A powerful training model would be for directors and teachers to attend trainings as a team, allowing time for collaborating and discussing the execution of the new information. This establishes a cultural norm for the group; everybody is moving forward and enhancing the outcome for the children. The power of this common language is evident with increased success for children and families.

Strategies for Reaching *All* Providers

How will you reach teachers who are not able to attend during the day? For those who cannot attend the group training, create alternatives, such as the following:

• During naptime, most centers and child care teachers can participate in on-site individual trainings.

• Evening or weekend trainings could provide an opportunity for teachers unable to attend trainings during the day. The person providing the training could work flexible hours and provide trainings after regular school hours. When that person also attends the trainings of the entire professional learning community, continuity and alignment of the trainings will transpire.

• A local cable channel or a high school production team could record and broadcast the trainings; this could fulfill a high school graduation requirement for a service project. Filming the trainings and creating DVDs or other formats for teachers to use could be one solution. Delivering the handouts or other materials electronically or posting them on a Web site, along with the DVD, ensures timely delivery. By broadcasting the training on a local cable channel and coordinating the time with typical naptime hours, teachers could view it at the same time from their own classroom.

- Satellite broadcasts would allow teachers the opportunity to be part of the discussions and to benefit from interactions with their peers.

- Explore technology that allows participants to call into a central phone number; they can then hear and participate in the training.

- Webinars, the format in which the visual content streams on the computer and the audio transmits over the telephone, are another option, depending on the technology and resources available.

Look within your community and identify a format that resonates with your group. One caveat: using technology could be a barrier to fostering relationships. The method or media is not as important as honoring teachers and their learning environments and spreading the word about the importance of early childhood.

Providing credits, educational units, or child care hours is a wonderful method to honor the work, time, and participation in the trainings. Connect with your state's child care quality rating system to arrange to have your trainings fulfill your state's requirements for quality training.

Connect with higher education. Barbara Bowman, from the Erikson Institute in Chicago, developed a program to offer degrees to teachers for participation and involvement in programs that are working to raise the quality of educational experiences for children. This could take the form of providing support and incentives toward obtaining their next degree. A local community or four-year college may be willing to collaborate on the degree program, especially if your system was data driven.

To implement this professional development system and format it with any topics that support your goal, do the following:

- Provide the research
- Inventory (find out what is already being done in the area)
- Continually increase the quality; don't just stay with the status quo
- Assess the gains
- Use this information to refine your work (friendly accountability)
- Keep repeating the cycle to fulfill your identified needs

Self-Reflection Leads to Your Next Step

Self-reflection, an often-ignored activity, is essential for learning from experiences. Dr. Lea Waters, from the University of Melbourne, described self-reflection as the "bridge between research and teaching" ("Reflecting on Reflection in Research and Teaching," 2009). This metacognitive activity facilitates continuous learning by providing time for teachers to contemplate their work with an eye toward improvement. It provides for multiple levels of knowledge and application of information; it is open-ended and honors the work each person does. It provides teachers with a means to evaluate their own progress. Without self-reflection, teachers are not able to understand and take the next steps. The reflection can be as simple as looking over a hierarchical checklist to determine a next step or as complex as completing an action plan or logic model. It could be describing what worked for you during a particular activity, what did not work, and what changes you will make next time.

Training evaluations, when taken seriously, are a form of self-evaluation. On the evaluation, include a question about new information learned and ask how it will be used on Monday morning. Doing a more extensive self-refection twice a year will give teachers a visual representation of their personal growth. In the fall, teachers should establish goals for their own growth; near the end of the school year, they can look at their goals, celebrate their growth, and establish new goals for the coming year. Teachers can put their new goals in a self-addressed envelope, with the coach mailing it to them at the end of the summer. This reminds them of the good work they have done as well as sets the stage for the upcoming school year with new goals.

Recording goals and growth for each teacher is a method for showing and celebrating successes. Resource E offers an example of a self-reflection form that can honor many levels of knowledge and skills, from acquisition of the skill to application to being ready to teach the skill. In order to build capacity from within our group, teaching others is the goal. This tends to solidify one's own skills and ensures that your group is not wholly dependent on one individual for everything. Ideally, teachers should be paired based on their skills; one teacher could be ready to teach a skill, while another is at the acquisition stage. Since the group is fluid, with new members joining, no one teacher remains a receiver of the information. Instead, the individual becomes the teacher for a new member; teaching others then solidifies his or her skills. In addition, the instructional coach can help provide the background information new members need for new learning.

Figure 4.3 Grow and Glow

Name: _____ Date: _____

Areas	Non-use I have not learned about this area yet; or I do not understand it.	Know I know the basic concept and I have tried a few activities.	Show I have used this frequently and still have some questions.	Grow I consistently use this and extend it into other areas of the curriculum. I would like more in-depth information.	Teach I am ready to collaborate and share information with others about this area. My doors are open for other to observe.
Structure					
Children's work displayed					
Well-defined routines					
Smooth transitions					
Centers for 45-60 min.					
Circle time interactive					
Small group time					
Phonological Awareness					
Rhyming activities					
Alliteration activities					
Segmenting activities					
Read Alouds					
2-3 readings of story					

Areas	Non-use I have not learned about this area yet; or I do not understand it.		Know I know the basic concept and I have tried a few activities.		Show I have used this frequently and still have some questions.		Grow I consistently use this and extend it into other areas of the curriculum. I would like more in-depth information.		Teach I am ready to collaborate and share information with others about this area. My doors are open for other to observe.	
Vocabulary words used										
Open-ended questions										
Story extenders used										
Print and Book Awareness										
Print rich environment										
Wall charts for children to read										
Letter wall used										
Talk about book parts										
Writing										
Writing center										
Writing materials in all centers										
Assessment										
Informally check student's skills often										

(Continued)

Figure 4.3 (Continued)

Areas	Non-use I have not learned about this area yet; or I do not understand it.	Know I know the basic concept and I have tried a few activities.	Show I have used this frequently and still have some questions.	Grow I consistently use this and extend it into other areas of the curriculum. I would like more in-depth information.	Teach I am ready to collaborate and share information with others about this area. My doors are open for other to observe.
Use assessment data to plan lessons					
My Goal:					

STEP 4 AT A GLANCE

- Provide professional development aligned to your goals
- Target professional development to the needs of your community
- Establish your professional development system
- Seek information to refine your work and strive for excellence
- Self-reflection leads to your next step

Next Step: After your success and celebration, your next step is to align and connect quality PreK with full-day kindergarten.

Step 5

Connect and Align Quality PreK to Kindergarten

There are a growing number of publications, articles, products, and software dedicated to assisting families and children through the transition process from preschool to kindergarten. This transition has such an impact on children's learning that it is part of the national Head Start and Title I requirements to raise achievement. We now have the National Early Childhood Transition Center funded by the Office of Special Education Programs to identify the best practices and strategies that assist children and families through this complex process. The alignment and connection of your quality community preschool programs to kindergarten is more than a transition of children and families. If done well, it becomes a strong instructional component of your PreK–3 system of support. Your goal is to maximize the benefits of a quality preschool education by aligning it to your kindergarten program's standards, assessments, curriculum, and instructional practices.

What Might the Future Be Like for the Children in Your Community If

- preschool children arrived at the kindergarten door with strong foundational skills?

- children and families did not have to learn a whole new set of classroom rules, routines, procedures, and standards?

- children could focus their cognitive energy on what is important for them to learn, while confident in their own ability to approach new experiences?

What If

- kindergarten teachers celebrated and built on the strengths of entering children to provide a quality learning experience?

- preschool and kindergarten teachers worked together as professionals sharing highly effective instructional strategies within a consistent structure and routine found in both the preschool and kindergarten classroom?

- teachers provided children with the additional practice opportunities they required in the areas that each child found challenging?

Connect Your Community Preschools to Kindergarten Programs

It is all about relationships; the preschool and kindergarten teacher partnership has tremendous benefits for children, families, and your school district. Identify the preschools that feed into your elementary schools as outlined in Step 2 and connect to your early childhood learning environments. Have your elementary principals establish a formal partnership with the community preschools that are within their boundaries *and* are a part of your PreK–3 efforts. These are the preschools that are examining research with your school district and are committed to your PreK–3 established goals. As you publicize the success of your PreK–3 system, your elementary principals will recruit new preschool members. Elementary principals and staff are quick to see the benefit of reaching children prior to kindergarten. Welcome these new partners to join your established leadership group and commit to full participation characterized by monthly professional development, use of consistent curriculum, and instructional practices and data review meant to adjust instruction. As a result, principals and staff will promote these preschools in your community and the quality of instruction these preschools provide. The goal is to have the elementary schools working with preschool staff and families to benefit children. The following are ways to expand your elementary school community to include children and families as equal partners prior to kindergarten:

- Have a list of partner preschools that are part of your PreK–3 efforts available for families and staff at every elementary school. Note that they are part of this PreK–3 effort to raise student achievement and provide families with a brief description of these preschools and their commitments to raise achievement.

- Actively pursue a professional relationship. Ask the principal and kindergarten teacher(s) to visit the preschools or arrange for an introductory meeting.

- Work with the early childhood providers to develop and disseminate a school calendar of family events that include young children at your school.

- Connect preschool family advocates and elementary interventionists or counselors with their shared families.

- Hold a spring preschool and kindergarten registration fair together. Offer preschool registration tables to each one of your preschool partners. Your preschool partners reap the benefits of increased enrollment in exchange for their participation in your PreK–3 efforts. Incoming kindergarten families meet their school principal and receive information and materials to work with their children over the summer.

- When possible, arrange for PE, library time, and music classes to include preschoolers.

- Expand your elementary PTA to include preschool families.

- Share resources that extend to preschool children, including building space when possible.

Provide Space for Preschool Programs in Your Elementary School

Use a Request for Proposal (RFP) process that stipulates that the preschool must be part of your leadership group, have insurance, and hire its own staff in exchange for reduced rent. The staff is to be an integral part of your system of support by participating in meetings, setting goals, and sharing resources. At the kindergarten transition, the families and children are already engaged and do not waste valuable time developing new relationships and learning new routines and procedures. The idea of shared resources will be expanded in Step 9.

The Role of the Elementary Principal

The role of the elementary principal is important in the connection and alignment of preschool and kindergarten. Unfortunately, we have witnessed schools that have preschools attached, but they are not a part of the elementary school. In some cases, the principal and teachers have not met the preschool staff or the children who will be attending their kindergarten the following year. What a missed opportunity for the children, families, and staff. Fortunately, more elementary school principals are learning about the value of early childhood and including their preschools. If you are a principal in a school that receives Title I funding, a requirement of the Comprehensive School Improvement Plan is to connect with your preschools. Where federal funds exist, such as Title I, Title I Part C (funding for migratory children), and Title III (funding for children to attain English language proficiency), there is a high probability that a federally funded preschool is close by to serve the needs of families with preschool-age children (e.g., a Head Start or Early Head Start program). Reach out to that preschool and invite them to be part of your district's early childhood leadership group. It is your job to be relentless in your efforts to collaborate with and promote early childhood education. Recognize your preschool teachers as part of your professional team. Advance your own professional knowledge by learning more about child development, brain research, and skills every child needs to know and do in the PreK–3 years. As a principal, you can either spend your limited resources trying to remediate deficits or prevent deficits by working with your preschools and families to provide children with a strong foundation. A valuable resource for principals is *Leading Early Childhood Learning Communities: What Principals Should Know and Be Able To Do* (National Association of Elementary School Principals and Collaborative Communications Group , 2005).

Make Your Preschools an Integral Part of Your Elementary Schools

Redefine elementary schools in your school district that have existing preschools attached to their buildings. Make these schools into PreK–3, PreK–5, or PreK–8 schools. Make the preschool staff an integral part of your school's comprehensive plan by including preschool staff in the following areas:

- Your building leadership team
- The development and implementation of your comprehensive school improvement plan
- Scheduling of activities
- Your child study team
- The staff roster, telephone trees, e-mail lists, and all school publications

Naval Avenue P–3 Early Learning Center

Naval Avenue P–3 Early Learning Center is an example of a school that previously housed K–5 classes, with an attached preschool. Their achievement was on a downward slope. The decision was made to reopen this school as a PreK–3 school with the expectation that it be used for research-based instructional practices and the alignment of preschool through the third grade. The fourth- and fifth-grade students were sent to another elementary school. The entire school staff, preschool through the third grade, was involved in the reopening of the school. In the first year, 94 percent of the kindergarten children were reading at benchmark levels, and the third-grade students exceeded the standard on the state assessment due to the schoolwide preschool-through-third-grade focus on achievement. Naval Avenue has a blended special education and Kitsap Community Resources Head Start preschool and a community Montessori preschool. Although the principal, John Welsh, does not supervise the community preschool teachers, he intentionally includes the preschool staff and knows the families and children. The PreK–3 teachers share assessment data and take part in schoolwide planning. The preschool children participate in monthly goal setting assemblies and access PE, music classes, and the library. The PTA includes parents of preschoolers. There is no need for formal transition plans from preschool to kindergarten, and little learning time is lost. Children and families already know the teachers in the building, and the staff is familiar with each child's strengths.

Align Your State's Early Learning and Development Benchmarks (Standards) With K–3 State Standards

Many states have their Early Learning and Development Benchmarks (Standards), from birth to age five, and K–12 Grade Level Expectations (Standards) online and available at no cost. Have your kindergarten teachers and preschool teachers compare and contrast the early learning benchmarks and kindergarten state standards and identify the implications for teaching and learning. Focus your alignment on preschool and kindergarten to articulate what every child needs to know and be able to do between the ages of three and six. Record the expectations and responsibilities of preschool and kindergarten programs. Take note that children develop skills along a continuum.

Include modifications and adaptations for children with disabilities. Be cautious that you do not underestimate children with disabilities. One of the many benefits of our work on building PreK–3 systems of support is the exceptional growth that many of our children with disabilities have made because of collaborative and focused efforts on the part of our community preschools, school districts, special education teachers, and support personnel. The National Early Literacy Panel is a valuable resource; it identifies interventions, family activities, and instructional practices that promote the development of children's early literacy skills from birth *through kindergarten* (*Developing Early Literacy: Report of the National Early Literacy Panel: A Scientific Synthesis of Early Literacy Development and Implications for Intervention*, National Institute for Literacy, 2008).

Develop an Assessment and Information Loop

A key component to building a PreK–3 system of support is to design and implement an assessment loop. It consists of a respectful review and use of data to make a difference in the lives of children. Incoming kindergarten children are assessed, and the information is used to "loop back" to the preschool programs and "loop forward" to the kindergarten programs. Both programs are adjusting their instruction to serve the children entering their programs. It is helpful to select nationally recognized universal screening instruments as well as other early childhood measures that provide you with the level of detail you require to make program decisions. Fortunately, the field of early childhood assessment is wide open, and we look forward to the development of quality assessments that are easy to administer and provide us with specific information on how children are progressing *and* how we can match our instruction and programs to better meet their needs.

Expand and align your data collection system to modify and adjust your preschool programs and instruction so that more children reach your established goal. Second, modify and adjust your kindergarten instruction to celebrate and build on the foundational skills that children come to you with. Last, partner with your preschools to close the gap in areas where children need additional practice or intensive support services.

Here are some successful strategies to build an assessment loop that meets the needs of your own community:

- Create an opt-out information and permission letter to send home to the families of incoming kindergarten children. These children are feeding into your kindergarten from your partner preschools. Have the letter signed by the school district and sent from the preschool. Publicize the good news that your district and the preschool are working together to provide children with a strong foundation prior to kindergarten.

- Assess incoming kindergarten children with an agreed-upon assessments, or universal, screener. We have found that it is important to wait at least three weeks into the school year to assess. Many children have difficulty that first month learning how to function in a large group in a new setting. We want children to feel comfortable and present their best efforts.

- In your early childhood leadership group, look at the overall results and percentages of children who participated in the partnership community preschools compared with children who came to kindergarten from other environments. Your group can then do the following:
  - Celebrate and record your successes.
  - Determine next steps.
  - Revise your instruction and plan your next series of monthly professional development staff trainings based on the needs of children and staff.
  - Take a look at the Recognition and Response (R&R) program. This is an excellent way to look at your preschool system and make adjustments. R&R is the preschool version of Response to Intervention, or RTI (Horowitz & Whitmire, 2008).

- At the kindergarten level, look at your data and the information provided on children from your preschool partners. One way to accomplish this is through a data-sharing meeting implemented at the school or district level. If done in the spring, the preschool leads with its data, and the kindergarten team would then have the information needed to adjust its program for the incoming children. If done in the fall, both the preschool and the kindergarten teachers have the opportunity to exchange information and make the necessary program adjustments. Some suggestions for data sharing are as follows:

- ○ Respectfully review data with the family, grade level teachers, and support staff to celebrate successes.
- ○ Determine the next steps for adjusting your instruction.
- ○ Seek professional development or job-embedded coaching to equip teachers with the tools they require to meet the needs of children.
- ○ Response to Intervention (RTI) is a valuable expanded process that enables you to look at your system and meet the needs of more children.

• Widely publish and celebrate the growth your preschool and kindergarten group has made; advertize it in the local paper, on the district Web site, at school board presentations, and at community-wide events.

• Use your data to set new goals or adjust time lines. Success is contagious, and those who remained on the sidelines to observe this new collective effort will now want to join. This continues to build your community PreK–3 system of support.

Align Curriculum and Instructional Practices

Align the curriculum and your instructional practices to support children's learning and development from preschool to kindergarten. Think about key concepts, instructional strategies, and research on child development as a PreK–3 continuum, rather than just skills you teach at preschool and kindergarten. Select core curriculum, supplemental materials, and instructional strategies that can be applied across early childhood (PreK–3), and make this part of your comprehensive school plan.

Alphabetic Principle Example

In one community preschool program that we worked with, the teacher used the adopted preschool curriculum that was aligned to our K–3 standards. This included teaching the alphabetic principle to the three- and four-year-olds. The toddler teacher in that same program appropriately extended the alphabet format and alphabet song from the curriculum to include her toddlers. The children were able to build on this first successful introduction to the letters as they progressed to the next level of alphabetic principle offered in preschool. Being already familiar with the format and the pleasurable activities and songs appropriate to toddlers, they were able to use their cognitive energy for new learning.

Curriculum and Supplemental Materials

Here are a few examples of alignment that will support the gains your children have made and continue their learning and development. Align your core and supplemental curriculum horizontally and vertically. Form agreements on what research-based programs will give your children the greatest probability of success. Record and disseminate your curriculum throughout your district; Title I and Head Start departments will assist you in this task. It is extremely difficult to make use of the current best practices and systems of support when you have not established agreements on a strong core and supplemental materials. Your teachers will be all over the board in terms of attempting to design effective interventions and supports. Recognition and Response (R&R) at the preschool level and Response to Intervention (RTI) at the K–12 level are two highly effective systems. They both require alignment of standards and assessments, progress monitoring, core and supplemental programs, and instructional practices. The following are some examples of curriculum that span preschool through third grade.

Handwriting Without Tears Program

Handwriting Without Tears, developed by Jan Z. Olsen, occupational therapist, is a program that starts in preschool and continues to build into elementary school to help children build handwriting skills.

Thinking Maps, Inc.: Visual Thinking Tools That Get Results

Thinking Maps are visual-verbal graphic organizers based on children's thinking and learning processes (Hyerle, 1995). Laura Kohn, at the New School, in Seattle, Washington demonstrated how effective the use of Thinking Maps was when used at a PreK–2 school. Naval Avenue P–3 Early Learning Center learned this concept from the New School and made it part of their schoolwide achievement plan.

Use of Schoolwide Thinking Maps, Preschool Through Third Grade

The teachers at Naval Avenue analyzed trends using the third-grade state assessment data to look for concepts that their children struggled with consistently. For example, the third-grade literacy skill of compare and contrast is a concept that is critical for all content areas and domains. By problem-solving together, the PreK–3 teachers realized that an underlying skill is the concept of "same and different." The teachers used the visual organizer Double Bubble, from Thinking Maps, to teach all PreK–3 children. All grade levels, including preschool programs in that building, had children proudly display their best Double Bubbles up and down the hallways. At the end of one year, their third-grade class demonstrated significant gains in this area. Carol Cummings, in her book Winning Strategies for Classroom Management, *(Cummings, 2000) uses this and other graphic organizers to teach children how to problem-solve and set goals, a critical element for self-efficacy.*

Figure 5.1 Preschool Adaptation of Schoolwide Use of Thinking Maps

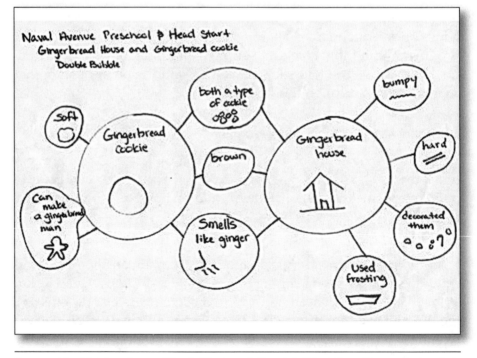

Source: Ms. Katrina Jones, Head Start and Special Education Team, Bremerton, Washington.

Instructional Practices

Instructional practices equip educators with the tools they require to support children's learning and align their teaching practices. Examples include the following:

Current Neuroscience (Brain) Research

• Current Neuroscience (brain) research translates into practical teaching and learning strategies that support children's learning. Carol Cummings, Judy Willis, and others have written several books using current brain research to differentiate curriculum and prepare the optimal learning environment for children.

Schoolwide Behavioral Support Systems

• Building a positive schoolwide behavioral support system is another instructional practice that will benefit PreK–3 children and support your mutual goals. Dr. Jeff Sprague has done extensive work in this area and offers practical strategies in *Best Behavior: Building Positive Behavior Support in Schools* for staffs to create positive behavioral support systems (Sprague, 2004).

Consistent Routines and Procedures

• Consistent routines and procedures allow children to engage in higher-level thinking and develop relationships, rather than spending their time trying to learn a new structure.

• *CHAMPs: A Proactive and Positive Approach to Classroom Management*, by Randy Sprick, Mickey Garrison, and Lisa Howard (1998) details a schoolwide approach that will benefit all your PreK–3 children.

Vocabulary Development

• Vocabulary development and building background knowledge are other building blocks that support all areas of children's learning.

• Exploring the work of Isabelle Beck, Steven Stahl, and Robert Marzano will provide you with ways to teach and enhance children's vocabulary development. Specific vocabulary-building strategies during "read alouds" will help your preschool and kindergarten teachers maximize the time they have with children.

• Examine and select critical math vocabulary. Joan D. Martin and Vicki C. Milstein have included one hundred math words that are appropriate to use and teach during the PreK–K years (Martin & Milstein, 2007).

STEP 5 AT A GLANCE

- Connect your community preschools to their elementary schools' kindergarten partners
- Examine the role of the elementary principal
- Make your preschools an integral part of your elementary schools
- Align your state's Early Learning and Development Benchmarks (Standards) with the K–3 state standards
- Develop an assessment and information loop
- Align curriculum and instructional practices that support children's PreK–3 learning and development

Next Step: Maximizing the benefits of full-day kindergarten.

Step 6

Maximize the Benefits of Full-Day Kindergarten

Advantages

The gift of time is the greatest benefit gained from offering full-day kindergarten. It is the only time in a child's educational career where we can literally double the amount of instructional time without taking something else away. This is wonderful news considering time is of the essence. Several longitudinal studies have shown us that "children who are poor readers at the end of first grade almost never acquire average-level reading skills by the end of elementary school" (Torgesen, 2004). This means we cannot wait; we must provide students with the skills they need early in their education. We also know from Torgesen's research that "given the results of a number of intervention studies, we can say with confidence that if we intervene early, intensively, and appropriately, we can provide these children with the early reading skills" needed to prevent them from experiencing academic failure (Torgesen, 2004).

Students come to us with a variety of skills and challenges. There never seem to be enough hours in the school day to meet everyone's needs. Unfortunately, the lack of time often requires educators to make very hard choices. This often results in taking time away from other academic or specialist areas in order to add intervention time. The areas that are most often compromised are ones that we can all agree are valuable, such as PE, music, library time, art, writing, science, or social studies. Many schools offer before- and afterschool programs as a way to increase instructional time, but then the problem becomes finding the extra funding, staff, transportation, and ways to entice students to attend the programs outside of their school day. This is why it is so critical that you take advantage of the opportunities offered by full-day kindergarten. If you are in a position to influence your school district into providing a full-day kindergarten, talk to the school superintendent, directors, and the school board to make it a reality for your children. The following research can support your proposal:

- Studies show that students in full-day kindergarten "outperformed their half-day kindergarten peers through Grade 3 in the areas of reading, mathematics, handwriting, spelling, and English" (Plucker & Zapf, 2005).

- Students who attended full-day kindergarten "earned higher grade point averages than their half-day kindergarten peers in Grades 6–8" (Plucker & Zapf, 2005).

- Full-day kindergarten students had higher test scores in Grades 3, 5, and 7 than their half-day kindergarten counterparts (Plucker & Zapf, 2005).

- A 2002 Montgomery County Public Schools study in Maryland "confirmed that children in free and reduced-price lunch and ESOL programs had the greatest rate of improvement compared to the half-day kindergarten program" (Brewster & Railsback, 2002), showing that full-day kindergarten works well for all children but has the greatest impact on those that need it the most.

National Trends

Despite the advantages offered by full-day kindergarten, it is not required or even offered in most states. "Currently, kindergarten attendance is mandatory in only 12 states, and only two states require children to attend full-day kindergarten" (School Library Journal, 2008). Even the very definition of full-day kindergarten varies from state to state. Kristi Kauerz's study shows that "while one state (Illinois) defines full-day kindergarten as four hours per day, three other states (Alabama, Louisiana, and Oklahoma) require six hours per day. While one state (Wisconsin) defines full-day kindergarten as 1,050 hours per academic year, another state (Florida) requires only 720 hours per year"

(Kauerz, 2005). Regardless of how many hours a day or how many days a year the programs are required to meet, the good news is that the "percentage of kindergartners enrolled in full-day programs has more than doubled, increasing from 28 percent of all kindergartners in 1977 to 65 percent of all kindergartners in 2003" (Child Trends Data Bank, 2003). A well-designed full-day kindergarten maximizes the instructional benefits for the children in your community and can have a positive impact on the rest of their educational career.

How to Design a Full-Day Kindergarten

Create a full-day kindergarten program that is targeted and intentional so that the gift of this extra time is not wasted. Districts can obtain lasting gains in student achievement by designing a kindergarten that is consistent across the district and aligning it with preschool and first-through-third grades. Key components in a strong full-day kindergarten include focused goals, consistent curriculum, and suggested schedules with time dedicated for math and reading instruction (whole-group, small-group, and activity centers). Also find ways to incorporate intervention, assessment, and accountability systems.

When progressing from a half-day kindergarten schedule to a full-day schedule, many districts make the mistake of simply stretching out the day. The lasting benefits of full-day kindergarten will fade out if schools and school districts do not plan carefully. The *fade-out effect* is a term used to describe a phenomenon in which the initial gains achieved by attending a high-quality preschool and full-day kindergarten eventually fade out through first, second, and third grades (Kauerz, 2006). Many schools have trouble in their first year of implementation because they fail to capitalize and plan for their additional learning time. Instead, they may fill the time with added snack times, nap time, recesses, or just slow down their pacing because they now have more hours in the day. In a time of increased accountability and decreased funding, view full-day kindergarten as a precious commodity and capitalize on this opportunity.

Developing a Planning and Implementation Team

The first step in building a strong full-day kindergarten program is to develop a dedicated planning and implementation team. This team will be responsible for many important tasks like developing goals, reviewing research, conducting a curriculum-adoption process, scheduling the day, and measuring results. They will also be responsible for reviewing and revising the program with input from the kindergarten teachers once it is operational.

The planning team could consist of key stakeholders such as the following:

- School board members
- District office administrators
- Curriculum and instruction director
- Title I director
- Building principals
- Kindergarten teachers from each school
- District Teachers on Special Assignment (TOSAs) and instructional coaches
- Preschool partners and child care providers

It is important that your planning team have broad representation. This will create an increased buy-in and foster a collaborative environment. When moving to a full-day kindergarten schedule for the first time, it might also be beneficial to have representatives from the transportation and food service departments, as well as community child care providers. This might seem unusual, but when a district moves from two half-day kindergarten programs to one full-day program it will impact all of these groups.

The following are some district planning team considerations:

- Bus drivers may lose their mid-afternoon bus runs, which could result in a cut in pay or loss of jobs.
- Child care providers may lose their half-day children, which could result in a loss of revenue.
- Food service staff will have to serve more students now that the kindergarten students will stay for lunch. Kindergarten students may have difficulty finding their lunch cards and memorizing their account numbers. Loading and carrying their trays independently without spilling will be another challenge.
- Recess supervision staff will have more students on the playground and a wider age range to oversee with kindergarten students staying all day.

Many schools fail to consider these details. Prior planning will provide children with a smooth and efficient start to their school year.

Developing Goals for the Program

When your team gathers for the first time, it is essential that they establish broad-range goals. Without a clear vision and specific goals, your team runs the risk of losing focus. We talked about developing goals for your preschool group in Step 3. Your team could begin with the same types of goals when moving to a full-day kindergarten program for the first time or when including an existing full-day program into a complete PreK–3 system. If your planning team wants to keep it simple, the goals could be (1) to increase the number of children entering first grade with foundational reading skills and (2) to decrease the number of children with learning difficulties associated with reading. These same goals can be used to increase math, writing, and social skills. You can develop different goals than those suggested here but keep them child-centered and guided by research based on best practices. We suggest starting with reading skills if you are developing a program for the first time because literacy is so critical to later academic success. You will also have a greater likelihood of success if you keep it simple your first year.

Using Research to Drive the Process

Your planning team will want to ensure that the goals they select are grounded in research and the best practices. Basing decisions on research will serve your team well; it will save time and keep your team focused on the goals. The planning team should develop a strong knowledge base regarding current research on effective instructional practices, neuroscience classroom management, social and emotional development, assessment, and data use. Your team must also be knowledgeable about the needs of incoming kindergarten students. It is important to recognize and capitalize on the strengths of the children and plan for their needs. When your team has this background information available to them, they can plan their program more effectively. Careful examination and use of data will create a high-quality kindergarten that is responsive to the children and families in your community.

Core Curriculum Selection Process for Your Kindergarten (K–3) System

The curriculum and instructional practices you adopt for use in your full-day kindergarten program will play a crucial role. They are key components to providing consistency and a common language across your school and district. You will want to select a curriculum that is research based, aligned to state standards, and meets the needs of the students in your community.

Benefits of Having a Core Curriculum

Some districts try to forgo adopting core curriculums at the kindergarten level because of budget constraints or philosophical reasons. However, without a common curriculum, the program may lack the consistency and intensity needed to make gains that will not fade out. Comprehensive core programs that are research based and validated provide teachers with the tools they need to teach whole-class and small-group instruction as well as enable them to offer individual support for students who struggle. Core programs offer consistent scope and sequence guides (showing the skills that the program covers); they can be used to align skills within and across grade levels. Solid core and intervention programs aid in the ability to modify and adapt curricula for children with special needs. Core curricula also lend themselves to other key ingredients in combating fade-out, like pacing maps (that align the skills to be taught with the district calendar, providing a suggested pace of instruction). Pacing maps support complete coverage of the material and help teachers avoid gaps in the instructional sequence from grade to grade. Common core and intervention programs also support cohesive staff development and a common language among practitioners. Strategies for avoiding fade-out will be discussed in Step 8.

Curriculum plays a powerful role in the overall effectiveness of a good kindergarten program. The article "Improved Early Reading Instruction and Intervention" notes that "a strong, core reading curricula—consistent with the research consensus on effective reading instruction and delivered by knowledgeable teachers—is essential for all students" (American Federation of Teachers, 2008). It is not only important to have strong core curricula but to have alignment between the curriculum levels. For the sake of simplicity, it is preferable to have the same curriculum from preschool through third grade. This provides a seamless transition from grade to grade, a more cohesive scope and sequence, and offers consistent routines and procedures. There are a multitude of districts across the nation that use programs in the primary grades that are different from those used in the intermediate grades; however, not all curricula are as strong as they need to be in the primary grades. The Institute for the Development of Educational Achievement at the University of Oregon reports that "schools often ask whether the adoption should be K–6 or whether a K–3/4–6 adoption is advisable. Ideally, there would be consensus across Grades K–6; however, it is imperative to give priority to how children are taught to learn to read. Therefore, kindergarten and first grade are critical grades and should be weighted heavily in adoption decisions. This may entail a different adoption for Grades 4–6" (Simmons & Kame'enui, 2003).

If you select a different curriculum for preschool than for Grades K–3, or if Grades 3–6 use a different curriculum than PreK–2, you will need to do the work of aligning the curriculum levels. Use the following steps to guide you:

1. Gather the scope and sequence chart for each of the core curricula.

2. Analyze and align the scope and sequence chart vertically to determine if there are any gaps in the skills covered between the programs from year to year.

3. Examine the routines, procedures, and materials from the different curriculums. Take note of similarities and differences. Some programs may perform activities differently, but the activities have the same purpose. Establish bridge activities or teaching that can be used to transition students from one program to the next.

4. Create an alignment document for your teachers that
   - identifies and fills the gaps in skills taught by each program,
   - has a plan that outlines what each grade level will need to teach to fill the gaps, and
   - explains the activities and teaching strategies that teachers will need to use to bridge the programs in order to provide a seamless transition from one program to the next.

If you have not adopted a core curriculum, you can use the curriculum selection process outlined in Step 3. Many supports are available online if you need guidance for reading adoptions. You can consult *A Consumer's Guide to Evaluating a Core Reading Program Grades K–3: A Critical Elements Analysis* (Simmons & Kame'enui, 2003). The Florida Center for Reading Research's *Guidelines for Reviewing a Reading Program* is another excellent resource. When selecting a math curriculum, teams can consult the *2008 Final Report of the National Mathematics Advisory Panel* for guidance on the components of an effective mathematics program.

Low- to No-Cost Options

If you do not have the funds at this point to secure a core reading and math program, you can follow the steps listed below to establish some common expectations and procedures vertically and horizontally in your district.

1. Conduct a review of current research and best practices

2. Review state and district standards as well as the demographic variables for your particular district

3. Conduct a strength-based inventory of what teachers are already doing

4. Review your assessment data to determine student needs

5. Create core materials, activities, and instructional practices that are aligned to your standards and demographic needs

6. Develop or purchase supplemental materials that provide additional learning opportunities

7. Establish consistent routines and instructional procedures

Developing Daily Schedule Expectations

Once you have selected the core curricula, the next critical step is to plan the daily schedule. Take advantage of the extra hours of instruction that full-day kindergarten offers. Be intentional and plan the year for the students you are getting not for the students you have had in the past. A key factor to combating the fade-out effect is to adjust instructional practices each year to build on success and meet the needs of the incoming students. This helps prevent a "business as usual" model. Specific strategies will be covered in detail in Step 8.

Scheduling out blocks of time for core subjects is the best place to start when developing the overall daily schedule. Many districts require a ninety-minute reading block and sixty-minute math block; the amount of time spent per subject is not arbitrary. There is a body of evidence in reading research that "repeatedly points toward TIME. It shows that students need a minimum of ninety minutes of uninterrupted reading instruction per day in order to develop sufficient reading development, the goal being to read on grade level" (Gumm & Turner, 2004). In addition to appropriating sufficient time for core subjects, districts must also take into account the unique strengths and needs of your community.

Consider the following essential components when building the daily schedule for your full-day kindergarten program.

- **Targeted vocabulary and oral language:** It is important that your full-day kindergarten programs also include strategies to increase vocabulary, domain knowledge, and oral language development. This is especially important if your district serves large numbers of students who come from low socioeconomic environments or speak a second language. "Such knowledge could be conveyed through read-alouds, well-conceived vocabulary instruction, and a variety of cumulative activities that immerse children in a word and world knowledge" (Hirsch, 2003).

- **Multiple joyful practice opportunities:** Learning new information comes easily for some students, but others will need multiple repetitions. There are three effective ways to increase the number of multiple joyful practice opportunities that students receive throughout their school day:
    - **Brisk pace:** Maintaining a brisk pace during instruction time will provide the teacher with more time in the lesson to offer additional practice opportunities to each student.
    - **Increase time on task:** This approach increases the amount of time that students are focused and engaged in the learning activities.
    - **Learning centers:** Learning centers are a wonderful way to provide students with multiple joyful practice opportunities. Centers need to target the skills learned during teacher-directed instruction time.

A Note on Learning Centers

Learning centers provide students with the opportunity to practice learned skills in a fun and engaging way. Learning centers should be targeted on the concepts students have learned and should provide them with a way to practice and generalize those skills across settings. You can use learning centers that come with your current curriculum, purchase them through educational vendors, or create them using ideas from books, Web sites, or magazines. Learning center resource options include the following:

- Lakeshore Learning Center Kits
- Florida Center for Reading Research Student Activity Centers
- Early Reading First Classroom Kits by Learning Resources

- LeapFrog PreK/Kindergarten Leapster Kits
- *Phonics From A to Z: A Practical Guide Grades K–3* by Wiley Blevins
- *Phonemic Awareness in Young Children: A Classroom Curriculum* by Marilyn Jager Adams

Core Instruction and Implementation

You have established the goals, selected a curriculum, and scheduled the day to maximize the benefits of full-day kindergarten. Keep in mind that an effective core curriculum is designed to meet the needs of approximately 80 percent of your students. This requires a commitment on the part of all of your kindergarten teachers. Commitment is not complacency; it is utilizing all of your resources, passion, and expertise to help children meet their full potential. A structured curriculum allows students to focus their learning and teachers to receive the tools they require to do this difficult work. Encourage teachers to infuse their own personalities and unique teaching styles within the structure of the curriculum.

The Role of Intervention and Assessment

As mentioned earlier, our students come to us with a variety of skills and challenges. Once the full-day kindergarten program is up and running, the team can loop back and add additional levels of support. One of these levels of support needs to focus on intervention. Two of the most effective systems to meet the needs of students are multitier instructional models and the Response to Intervention model. Both of these models are discussed in detail in subsequent steps. Be sure to select intervention systems that meet your students' unique needs and provide you with the highest probability of success.

A successful intervention system should do the following:

- Use research-based and validated supplemental programs
- Target skills the student is lacking
- Monitor to determine effectiveness

The Role of Assessment

Assessment plays an important role in the design and effectiveness of a PreK–3 system. It is critical to have an assessment loop that enables data sharing from the preschool teachers up to the kindergarten teachers and then sends kindergarten data back to preschool teachers. We will discuss in the next step how that same assessment loop can be extended to share data between kindergarten teachers and first-grade teachers and beyond. Data helps build a dynamic system of support by providing the information required to respond to the immediate needs of students; it allows us to determine if we are providing effective instruction at the classroom, school, and district level.

Universal screeners are a valuable tool in a PreK–3 system because they allow us to compare our students to others across the nation. Universal screeners are typically given three or four times per year to every student in a particular grade level. Some examples of universal screeners include:

- DIBELS (Dynamic Indicators of Basic Early Literacy Skills)
- AIMSweb
- FAIR (Florida Assessment for Instruction in Reading)

They provide unbiased data, independent of the core curriculum, for determining if our students are acquiring the critical early reading skills and if they are able to generalize those skills to other tasks. Universal screeners provide us with a quick, efficient way to screen students and determine who is at risk. Diagnostic tests provide another level of assessment; they help us dig deeper to determine the exact skills our students are missing. You can give these tests to all students or only to the students identified by the universal screener as being at risk. Use the data gleaned from diagnostic tests to adjust instruction and target the exact skills students are missing. Diagnostic test data is also helpful in developing goals for supplemental support during double-dose instruction time (providing an additional session of targeted instruction that focuses on the skills needed by the student). To determine whether the program needs to change and whether interventions are positively affecting student achievement, you can use progress-monitoring assessments. Progress-monitor the students identified to be at-risk by the universal screener every two to four weeks. Remember, it is important to progress-monitor at the instructional level. Curriculum-based measures (CBM) are also helpful in determining the skills a student is missing; they show if the students are learning the material taught in the core curriculum.

Assessment data are also very useful at the district level; use data to evaluate the effectiveness of the full-day kindergarten program itself. Offering a full-day kindergarten instead of half-day kindergarten is a costly investment. District and community members will want to know if it is making a significant difference. Quality data collection and instructional consistency across the district will enable district office administrators to isolate the variables and track cohorts to determine which instructional practices are effective and which are not. The following is a list of strategies we have found helpful:

- Keep the full-day kindergarten programs in your district consistent so you can isolate the variables
- Use data collected from universal screeners to examine and share achievement in multiple ways (with individual students, the classroom, the school, and the district as a whole)
- Collect data reliably and consistently to track cohorts and identify trends (this will be discussed in Step 8)
- Celebrate the successes

Data Sharing

Establishing a culture of data sharing and friendly accountability will help you build a strong system yielding lasting results that will not fade out in subsequent years. Consistent with your preschool system, the goal is to create a culture to collect, analyze, and share data. Research tells us that using and sharing assessment data is a common practice used in the most effective schools (Cotton, 1995). Data sharing can feel intimidating to many educators at first. They are often worried that their peers or administrators will judge them if their student's achievement results are not meeting expectations. Establish data-sharing systems to build trust and open communication among staff.

Teachers report greater differentiation of instruction, greater collaboration among faculty, increased sense of teacher efficacy, and improved identification of students' learning needs as outcomes of data use. Administrators and principals report that working with data support personnel leads to more widespread feelings that instructional practice should be open, observed and discussed, as opposed to something that happens behind closed doors (van Barneveld, 2008).

Friendly Accountability

The importance of the work that we are doing to improve the lives of children demands accountability. The advantages of developing a friendly accountability system in preschool outlined in Step 4 are also important at the kindergarten level and up through third grade. Here are some examples of friendly accountability systems:

- **Learning Walks:** Learning walks are a professional-development opportunity that enables teachers to learn from one another. As mentioned in earlier chapters, many different versions of this type of professional development have emerged over the last few years. Conducting staff development opportunities like learning walks within a single school or across the district provides teachers with a chance to observe classrooms in the grades that precede and follow the grade they teach. For example, kindergarten teachers can go into preschool and first-grade classrooms to see the alignment (or lack thereof) between the grades. Teachers can also walk through classrooms of their colleagues who teach the same grade as they do to see new ideas and strategies. This type of staff development allows educators to refine and improve their skills through peer observation and aligned staff development. In addition to the instructional benefits, learning walks can also provide a certain level of accountability. They help teachers see how important pacing and teaching core and supplemental programs with fidelity are in terms of student achievement. It also gives teachers a chance to see how unique each classroom can be, despite having consistent materials and expectations.

- **Pacing Maps:** Establishing pacing charts for your core curriculum will assist in avoiding gaps in instruction from grade to grade. To create pacing maps, align the scope and sequence of the program with the district calendar. Then align the pacing map to the pace of the students who are performing at grade level. Some student groups will need to progress more quickly or more slowly than the recommended pace, but the pacing maps give educators a target.

- **Curriculum Maps:** These maps list the approved core and supplemental programs that will support students who are performing above, at, or below standard. Develop a curriculum map for all grades within the PreK–3 system. Having a curriculum map gives teachers and schools curriculum options while at the same time maintaining the consistency that benefits our students. This is especially important if your district has high internal mobility. Students will not lose valuable instruction time or have gaps in their learning if you maintain consistency throughout the district as much as possible.

- **Publicizing and Celebrating Your Results:** Research shows that effective schools "establish award programs for schools, administrators, teachers, and students and take a visible role in recognizing excellence" (Cotton, 1995). They also "make certain that district monitoring of school operations and improvement efforts is accompanied by recognition of successes" (Cotton, 1995). Implementing activities that publicize and celebrate will honor the hard work of the students, teachers, and administrators in your district. It is also important to share your successes with your local community.

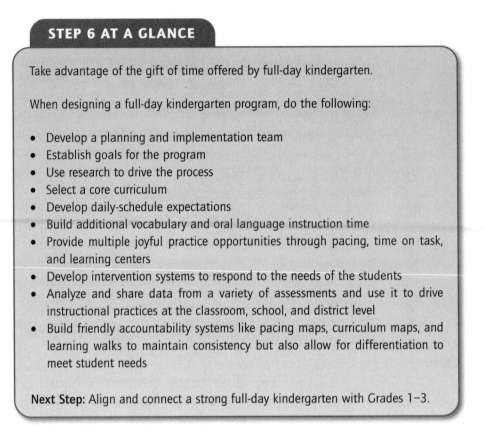

STEP 6 AT A GLANCE

Take advantage of the gift of time offered by full-day kindergarten.

When designing a full-day kindergarten program, do the following:

- Develop a planning and implementation team
- Establish goals for the program
- Use research to drive the process
- Select a core curriculum
- Develop daily-schedule expectations
- Build additional vocabulary and oral language instruction time
- Provide multiple joyful practice opportunities through pacing, time on task, and learning centers
- Develop intervention systems to respond to the needs of the students
- Analyze and share data from a variety of assessments and use it to drive instructional practices at the classroom, school, and district level
- Build friendly accountability systems like pacing maps, curriculum maps, and learning walks to maintain consistency but also allow for differentiation to meet student needs

Next Step: Align and connect a strong full-day kindergarten with Grades 1–3.

Step 7

Align and Connect a Strong Full-Day Kindergarten With Grades 1–3

By now your district has established connections with local preschools and you have a strong full-day kindergarten. All of this work will be for nothing if you do not focus on strategic alignment with Grades 1–3. Many districts celebrate the initial bump up in student achievement that preschool and full-day kindergarten offer, only to experience a fade-out by third grade. This is because districts fail to align and adapt the subsequent years to meet the needs of the incoming students. Remember, each grade level must plan for the students they are getting, not for the students they have had in the past. When schools follow a business-as-usual model, they will lose all of the gains achieved by preschool and full-day kindergarten. Specific steps to combat this fade-out effect in the context of your entire PreK–3 system will be discussed in Step 8.

Studies show that strong PreK–3 programs have several key components, including alignment, organization, and accountability (Graves, 2006). The *Early Childhood Longitudinal Study* (Watson & West, 2004) analysis showed that "children who experience PreK–3 components perform better in third grade than those who do not." Their analysis also demonstrates the importance of receiving multiple PreK–3 components over time. "Those who experience all components perform better than those who experience only half, and those who experience half perform better than those who experience none" (Graves, 2006). The National Head Start/Public School Early Childhood Transition Demonstration Study Project also reinforced "the cumulative power of key components in a PreK–3 strategy; the more components, the better children fare and achieve" (Graves, 2006).

Connect Your Full-Day Kindergarten to Grades 1–3

The Role of the Elementary Principal as an Instructional Leader

Principals of successful PreK–3 systems are instructional leaders who are skilled at curriculum and instruction as well as building management. They understand the importance of assessments and know how to analyze the data to improve instruction. They know what quality instruction looks like and work with teachers to implement the curriculum with fidelity. Ways to achieve this include the following:

- Setting and aligning schoolwide goals from PreK–5 (including them in the comprehensive school improvement plan)
- Providing opportunities for grade levels to team vertically
- Looking at data across grade levels to identify patterns
- Establishing joint professional learning communities and staff development
- Looking at research and discussing its implications and applications within and across each grade in the PreK–3 (or 5) system

If you are not at this level of instructional leadership as a principal, then surround yourself with a team that includes instructional coaches and grade-level teacher leaders. State-level resources might also be of assistance. Many states have experts in reading and assessment who would be willing to come to your school to help facilitate professional development opportunities.

More Than Connection: Make Full-Day Kindergarten an Integral Part

Principals of successful PreK–3 schools also find ways to unite and elevate the importance of their kindergartens. Unfortunately, there are still many kindergarten teachers across the country who feel like they are just an add-on to their school. This is unfortunate because in reality kindergarten plays a vital role in student achievement. Therefore, the principal must lead by helping other teachers in the building see that preschool and kindergarten provide the foundation upon which the rest of the child's education is built. Make kindergarten teachers an integral part of the school by doing the following:

- Including a kindergarten teacher on school leadership teams
- Including kindergarten in the planning and implementation of professional development
- Providing kindergarten with access to high-quality curriculum and materials
- Building kindergarten into the master schedule (providing access to specials, recesses, interventionists, Title I, and Special Education services)
- Elevating the importance of the kindergarten teaching position through the hiring and evaluation process, demonstrating that kindergarten instruction requires our best teachers

Align Your K–3 Standards

In the document "PK–3: What Is It and How Do We Know It Works?" Bill Graves reports that successful PreK–3 systems align their standards within and across grades (Graves, 2006). In Step 5, "Connect and Align Quality PreK to Kindergarten," we discussed how to align your Early Learning and Development Benchmarks/Early Childhood Standards to the K–3 standards. Now it is equally important to align your K–3 standards across grades. The intent of the learning expectations in state standards is to transition children or to provide seamless transition from grade to grade. However, most teachers will tell you that the process is not as seamless as one would hope. There are often gaps in the cognitive demand, the content covered from one grade to the next, or both. If you find this issue in your state standards, you will need to determine if your curriculum and pacing give the students enough practice to make this jump. If not, the staff will need to decide how they will close that gap. Which grade will be responsible for providing more practice opportunities and increasing the cognitive demand of the activities?

Another alignment issue that arises is in the content expectations themselves. In kindergarten the expectation might be for students to count to fifty, but by first grade they are expected to count to one thousand. Do your core math curriculum and your pacing map help you meet this rise in expectations? Are they aligned? If not, the staff will need to determine who will be responsible for closing the gap. Perhaps the kindergarten teachers will need to get their students to count up to one hundred, and first-grade teachers could take it from that point to one thousand. Being aware of the alignment within the standards themselves and how it correlates to your core curriculum and pacing expectations will help you avoid gaps in learning and provide a seamless transition from year to year for your students.

Align Your Assessment and Information Loop

Step 5 discussed creating an assessment loop between your preschool partners and your full-day kindergarten program. Now, you will repeat that same process between full-day kindergarten and Grades 1–3. The following are key components involved in developing an assessment loop.

Select Consistent Assessment Tools

The first step in creating an assessment loop is to make sure Grades K–3 are using the same assessment tools. Select a universal screener, a progress-monitoring tool, and a diagnostic-assessment instrument to use consistently in all grades. The use of consistent screening tools will be just as critical to the success of your PreK–3 system as having a core curriculum.

Establish Data Sharing and Storage Systems

The second step is to create a standard format for viewing and sharing data. Most schools find it easiest to use Excel spreadsheets. Using the same format will enable teachers to have discussions within and across grade levels. It allows staff to have focused discussions in a short amount of time because everyone knows how to read the data and analyze it.

You may choose to purchase a Web-based data analytics and storage program. These systems allow you to store, retrieve, disaggregate, and analyze data. Having access to this type of system will allow you to track the progress of all demographic groups, cohorts, and individual students.

Use the Data

It is important to create a data-driven culture in your PreK–3 system where staff members are all active participants in the respectful review and use of the data collected from the universal screener, the progress-monitoring tool, and the diagnostic assessment. Two major purposes of the data are as follows:

1. Use the data to make instructional decisions. Grade level teams can determine the need to adjust "walk to read" groups. (*Walk to read* refers to a system of providing leveled reading instruction within or across grade levels to meet the diverse instructional needs of students.) Response to Intervention teams can use it to determine if students would benefit from a double or triple dose of instruction. Also, individual teachers can use it to make changes in their instruction to meet the needs of the students in their class. Schools are able to use the data to determine their schoolwide intervention effectiveness.

2. Use the data to fight the fade-out effect. The sending grade can use the data to share the accomplishments and challenges of their students with the receiving grade. Schools who fail to share data vertically often see the results achieved by preschool and full-day kindergarten fade out in subsequent years. If the receiving teachers develop their instructional plan based on the data they receive on the incoming students, then they will be able to continue the trajectory of success. This handoff and adjustment process happens every year from one grade to the next. We will continue a discussion of this concept in greater depth in Step 8: Conquer the Fade-Out.

Align Curriculum and Instructional Practices That Support Children's K–3 Learning and Development

Many schools fall prey to the idea that once they select and implement consistent core curricula and assessments, they have completed their work. The fact is that this is when the real work begins. It is not enough to say that you use a universal screener or to say that you teach your core reading program. You must make sure that you are using those tools to maximize the benefits for the children. You can do this only by truly teaching the core program with fidelity and by using the assessment data to actually change instructional practices. Many teachers allow the curriculum to drive them. To take your school or district to the next level, you must show the teachers how to drive the curriculum. This does not mean that teachers should forgo fidelity by picking and choosing which elements of the program they want to use nor does it mean that they should be drastically changing the components of the program by supplementing materials that change the integrity of the curriculum. What it means is that teachers require ongoing high-quality staff development and coaching in order to know the core curriculum inside and out. They need the same level of intensive training on supplemental and intervention programs as they did for the core program. Once teachers reach this level of expertise with the curriculum, they will be able to use it as a framework that can be flexed and adjusted to meet the needs of their students. They will become skilled problem solvers, will teach to fidelity, and will become able to adjust their pacing and intensity. They will increase their level of explicitness by focusing on skills that students are missing and providing additional practice opportunities to meet those needs. Teachers will know how to incorporate approved supplemental programs when needed to repair their student's skill deficits. You will have greater success with your PreK–3 system if you establish a curriculum map for core and supplemental materials shared districtwide.

How to Align Your Core, Supplemental, and Intervention Programs

In order to align your core, supplemental, and intervention programs, follow these two steps:

1. Determine which core programs will be used for students who are above, at, slightly below, and significantly below grade level. Select programs that are research based and validated and best meet the needs of the students you serve. Remember to make sure your programs are aligned both vertically and horizontally.

2. Determine which supplemental programs will be used for students who are slightly below grade level or have targeted deficit areas. These programs should accelerate the student's learning, be research based, and have validated results. Categorize these programs by grade level and the skill areas they address so teachers can make tactical decisions.

In Step 5 we mentioned several instructional practices that will support children's learning and development. Expand those same practices through the third grade. Services and supports that span multiple grade levels provide a common language among the teachers and students in a school. They also make the transition from grade to grade easier for students. Thinking Maps (Hyerle, 1995) and Step Up to Writing (Auman, 2003) are examples of curricula used from the primary all the way to the secondary level. Programs like *Best Behavior: Building Positive Behavior Support in Schools* (Sprague, 2004) and *CHAMPs* (Sprick, Garrison, & Howard, 1998) are examples of programs that teach routines, procedures, and expectations that span across grade levels to provide consistency for students.

Tiered reading models and Response to Intervention are other systems that will help refine and take your PreK–3 efforts up a notch. Instituting a system like a tiered reading model, Response to Intervention, or both, in addition to all of the things we covered in this step, will help to streamline your system and make it stronger and more efficient.

Tiered Systems

Instituting a tiered model of instruction and a Response to Intervention system is an excellent way to connect and align resources to meet the needs of your students. A tiered model of instruction will help schools offer cohesive services that meet the needs of every student. A Response to Intervention system will provide you with a way to record students' progress and to analyze the effectiveness of your system. It also helps staff focus on the school's instructional system as a whole, as well as on individual student needs. "In multitiered models of service delivery, instruction is differentiated to meet learner needs at various levels. Several specific factors or dimensions help distinguish among interventions at the various tier levels. In general, a higher degree of specificity and intensity is associated with a higher tier of intervention" (Johnson, 2006). Sharon Vaughn states, "The 3-tier model (Texas Education Agency and the University of Texas System, 2004) is a way of thinking about instruction that emphasizes ongoing data collection and immediate intervention for students who need it. It is intended to include any research-based program that already incorporates additional intervention" (Vaughn, 2005).

A variety of tiered instructional models and Response to Intervention systems are available. Most tiered systems have three tiers, but there are systems that have four and five tiers. While the majority of tiered instructional models focus on reading, some are applicable for math and social skills or behavior. We have found the following to be useful:

- Texas's "3-Tier Reading Model" (Texas Education Agency and the University of Texas, 2004)
- The "Washington State K–12 Reading Model" (Washington State Office of Superintendent of Public Instruction, 2005)
- Jeff Sprague's "Best Behavior: Building Positive Behavior Support in Schools" (Sprague, 2004)
- Wayne Callender's "Response to Intervention Model" (Callender, in press)
- "Using Response to Intervention (RTI) for Washington's Students" (Washington State Office of Superintendent of Public Instruction, 2006)

Your district can follow one model or a combination of the models to develop a structural framework that will support your district in providing students with high-quality core instruction and intervention services.

In a three-tiered reading model, Tier I consists of ninety or more minutes of core reading instruction. The goal is that "in Tier I, school districts provide a foundation of curriculum, instruction, and school organization. This helps bring a large percentage of students (80%) to acceptable levels of proficiency" (Center for Educational Networking, 2006). Proficiency is determined by administering the benchmark screener at least three times per year. Give additional "digging-deeper" assessments to gather more in-depth information. Students remain in the Tier I core instruction group if they score in the benchmark, or no-risk, categories of the screener. Washington state sets a higher standard, stating that Tier I instruction should meet the needs of 85 percent or more of the students if the system is working correctly (Washington State Office of Superintendent of Public Instruction, 2005).

If students fall in the strategic, or some-risk, category on the universal screener, they qualify for Tier II services, which consist of thirty additional minutes of targeted instruction in addition to the ninety minutes of Tier I core instruction. The goal of Tier II is to provide targeted short-term interventions to students who responded poorly to the core instruction received in Tier I or who need more practice. Students in Tier II are tested using a progress-monitoring tool that is part of their universal screening assessment every two weeks. The students remain in Tier II until they are able to acquire the skills needed to score in the benchmark, or no-risk, range on the screener and to perform proficiently in Tier I core instruction without support. Students who need Tier II intervention are typically those who have a gap in their learning and need more instruction or practice on a targeted skill than the core program offers. Children receive Tier II in a small-group setting using explicit and systematic instructional techniques. You can teach this thirty-minute double dose using the supplemental curriculum materials from the core program itself. You could also create targeted preteach and reteach lessons that focus specifically on the skills the student needs. Using additional supplemental materials that are not part of the core is another option. However, when doing so schools need to make sure that the supplemental program aligns with the core program and that it is targeting the student's area of weakness. Putting students in a program that does not target their area of need is a great waste of time and resources. An example to illustrate this point would be if a student scored in the strategic range on the universal screener, and when giving an additional digging-deeper assessment, we discovered the student had multiple errors and gaps in the area of phonics. This student would be a good candidate for additional systematic phonics instruction targeting the specific sounds and blends the student is missing. However, we often see schools making the error of putting these types of students into a program during Tier II instruction that only targets fluency. The problem with this is that the student has so many errors and gaps in his or her learning that he or she would only be practicing errors and not working on the area of need, which is phonics. This only exacerbates the problem; the students continue to practice errors without hope of remediation in the very area of need. Tier II instruction should be needed by less than 10 percent of the student population (Washington State Office of Superintendent of Public Instruction, 2005).

Tier III instruction is reserved for the 5 percent of students who did not respond to interventions offered in Tier I and Tier II (Washington State Office of Superintendent of Public Instruction, 2005). These students scored in the intensive, or at-risk, range on the universal screener. They need intensive intervention that is very systematic, explicit, and of high intensity. When a student requires Tier III services, they often receive sixty additional minutes of instruction in addition to the ninety minutes of core Tier I instruction. The students who typically qualify for Tier III instruction are significantly behind their same-age peers. Some of the students in Tier III will benefit from receiving Tier I core instruction in addition to sixty additional minutes of intensive intervention in their areas of need. However, when students are more than two years below grade level, they often need a replacement core program. Most core programs are not designed to make up two-plus year's growth in one year's time. However, some intervention or replacement core programs are specifically designed to close the achievement gap between the struggling students and their peers in a short time. These programs have a placement test that assesses the students' present levels of performance and places them in the appropriate unit of instruction. Effective intervention or replacement core programs are mastery based and have flexible pacing schedules so students can move through the program as quickly as possible while showing mastery of essential skills.

Connect and Align
Resources to Focus on Your Goals

The last thing to consider when aligning your preschool and full-day kindergarten to Grades 1 through 3 is the alignment of resources. When you implement systems like the 3-Tier Reading Model or Response to Intervention, this connects and aligns your resources to better meet the needs of all students. We highly recommend that if you qualify for Title I services and meet the requirement for free and reduced lunch, that you become a schoolwide Title I program. This takes a year, but it will allow you greater flexibility in funding and allows you to focus on *all* students. Students with disabilities, those with limited English proficiency, and general-education students who are not meeting standards can all be served within your tiered intervention model and can receive additional services. This schoolwide approach helps you to align your resources and staff so that they are all working toward a common goal. We often see schools that have fragmented services because they are working in separate silos. Is this happening in your school? Do the general education, Title I, special education, and bilingual teachers team together? Do they have access to the same curriculum resources? Do they look at the same data? What about your paraeducators, AmeriCorps workers, and volunteers . . . have they been trained, and are they providing consistent and aligned instruction to your students? Be sure to ask these types of questions in your building. Find ways to create a schoolwide and districtwide PreK–3 support system with all staff working together to provide high-quality instruction for the students you serve.

STEP 7 AT A GLANCE

Connect Your Full-Day Kindergarten to Grades 1–3

- Set and align schoolwide PreK–3 goals
- Provide opportunities for grade levels to team vertically
- Look at data across grade levels to identify patterns
- Establish joint professional learning communities and staff development
- Look at research and discuss its implications and applications within and across grades
- Make full-day kindergarten an integral part of your school

Align Your Assessment and Information Loop

- Select consistent assessment tools
- Establish data-sharing and storage systems
- Use the data to make instructional decisions and fight the fade-out

Align Curriculum and Instructional Practices

- Select core and supplemental programs that are research based and validated
- Align the programs vertically and horizontally to each other and the standards
- Select curriculum and instructional practices that span multiple grades to provide consistency
- Implement a 3-Tier Reading Model

Connect and Align Resources to Focus on Your Goals

- Find ways to create schoolwide and districtwide intentional opportunities for all staff (special education, Title I, ELL [English Language Learners] and general education) to work together to provide high-quality instruction for students.

Next Step: Combat the fade-out.

Step 8

Conquer the Fade-Out

A growing number of studies caution educators and policy makers on investing their funding in early childhood education due to the possibility of a fade-out effect. This happens when the successful gains that children experience from a quality preschool and kindergarten start to diminish or *fade out* by third grade. This is not new information. In fact, in 1997, Robert J. Rossi and Samuel C. Stringfield (Rossi & Stringfield, 1997) spoke to the fade-out effect while also addressing the long-term positive impact of preschool intervention. Prior to that, Natriello, Pallas, and McDill warned of the need to build upon a solid preschool foundation while continuing to provide quality instruction: "Preschool intervention is more effective than school-age intervention at enhancing intellectual growth and improving student performance (Campbell and Ramey, 1989). However, a fade-out effect may occur if successive grades fail to build upon preschool influences and address age-specific needs" (Natriello, Pallas, & McDill, 1990).

In order to sustain the gains that you made by providing children with a strong quality preschool and kindergarten, you must be relentless in your fight against the fade-out effect. In our work, we made an extensive effort to create a strong PreK–3 system of support that builds on and sustains the gains that children have made. We examined and applied the research to ensure that the steps presented in this book incorporated the critical elements known to conquer the fade-out effect. We encourage you to examine these steps and current research on effective measures that combat the fade-out and apply these to your own community PreK–3 system of support. Do not rest on your success. Assume that your children will lose the gains they have made *unless* you formulate and implement a plan to aggressively counter the fade-out. Use or modify the implementation strategies outlined throughout this book and specifically those outlined here for your own community. Watch over your "own" children to ensure that they continue to move forward and acquire more complex skills.

Kristie Kauerz, a doctoral candidate at Columbia University, has done an excellent job of addressing three significant factors that will help you fight the fade-out effect: alignment of standards, curriculum, and assessment (Kauerz, 2006). We have embedded these three throughout our book and added to them to insulate your community efforts from the possibility of fade-out. These practical suggestions are based on our experiences and could be included in your strategic planning process. Our goal is to provide you with all the tools you require to ensure sustained success. In Step 5 and Step 7, we provided specific examples of how to align PreK with K and K–3:

- Align Early Learning and Development Benchmarks with K–3 standards and assessments
- Develop an assessment and information loop
- Align PreK–3 assessment
- Align core curriculum, supplemental materials, and instructional practices
- Connect and align resources to support your goals

In previous steps, we talked about the alignment of PreK–3 assessment. Progress monitoring of *all* children, including children who have reached benchmark or have demonstrated proficiency, is an effective strategy to combat the fade-out. If children start to slip back, you want to be able to adjust your instruction in time to get these children back on track. Sometimes in our attempts to help our most struggling students, we turn over the instruction of our higher-functioning children to our less-experienced teachers. When children are functioning at or above grade level, there may be a tendency to modify, expand, or enrich the curriculum for these students. It is important that any adjustments made to your instruction continue to be based on effective practices and are aligned to your curriculum. For example, when we discovered that our first-grade students were advancing midyear to the point of reading chapter books, we made sure that we purchased science and social studies extension books that aligned with the core curriculum and instruction. By keeping a careful watch on children who are functioning on either end of the spectrum and in between, you maximize the benefits for all children.

The Foundation for Child Development highlighted the work of Kristie Kauerz on alignment by addressing three critical areas: horizontal alignment, vertical alignment, and temporal alignment. We offer suggestions to expand and operationalize these key elements in your own community by pulling together the strategies embedded in each previous step to fight fade-out.

Teach the Conventional Reading Skills That Are Developed From Birth to Age Five

The first step to fighting the fade-out in the area of early literacy is to make sure that you are teaching the conventional reading and writing skills that are developed in the years from birth to age five *and* have a clear and consistently strong relationship with later conventional literacy skills. The *Developing Early Literacy* report of the National Early Literacy Panel (National Institute for Literacy, 2008) outlines six variables representing early literacy skills that had a medium to large predictive relationship with later measures of literacy development. "These six variables not only correlated with later literacy as shown by data drawn from multiple studies with a large number of children but also maintained their predictive power even when the role of other variables, such as IQ or socioeconomic status (SES), were accounted for." The six variables listed in the NELP report are the following:

1. Alphabetic Knowledge (AK): Knowledge of the names and sounds associated with printed letters.

2. Phonological Awareness (PA): The ability to detect, manipulate, or analyze the auditory aspects of spoken language (including the ability to distinguish or segment words, syllables, or phonemes), independent of meaning.

3. Rapid Automatic Naming (RAN) of letters or digits: The ability to rapidly name a sequence of random letters or digits.

4. RAN of objects or colors: The ability to rapidly name a sequence of repeating random picture-sets of objects (e.g., *cat, tree, house, man*) or colors.

5. Writing or writing name: The ability to write letters in isolation on request or to write one's own name.

6. Phonological memory: The ability to remember spoken information for a short period of time.

Have your leadership group inventory and review how much time you are spending teaching these important variables to children from preschool through kindergarten. The Early Literacy Panel also addresses five more literacy skills that were moderately correlated with at least one measure of later literacy development. This report will help your leadership group determine what is important for children to learn, the most effective instructional practices, and the implications for children's future.

Horizontal Alignment

Horizontal alignment is the process of linking standards, curriculum, and assessment within grade levels and across the entire district in your community. In Step 3: "Develop a Leadership Group" and Step 6: "Maximize the Benefits of Full-Day Kindergarten," we provided examples of ways to establish a research-based core curriculum that is shared by all community preschool partners and aligned with all grade levels, PreK–3, throughout the district and community. Curriculum maps are a method of achieving horizontal alignment and they outline grade-level specific core and supplemental curriculum to provide a consistent districtwide tiered-intervention approach for all children. When creating your own curriculum map for the purpose of horizontal alignment, be sure you involve grade-level teachers throughout your district. It will be important to provide as much detail as possible. For example, what is the best curriculum to use for core and replacement? What Tier II intervention programs work best to address a specific skill deficit? By being specific about the research-based curriculum, supplemental programs, and materials offered to the children in your school district, you ensure that all children receive exceptional intervention regardless of the school they attend. You will find that many teachers are eager to take on the responsibility of putting together a districtwide curriculum map. This is another way of "infusing each position with importance" and establishing broad-based support. Have someone knowledgeable in the field critique your curriculum map; curriculum people at the state level are a valuable resource.

It is important that all community preschool partners and grade-level teachers know what the goal is and the reasons that your community has prioritized this goal (positive impact on children) *and* that they are committed to working together to achieve the common goal(s). It only takes one or two individuals to deviate from your agreed-upon plan to disrupt your PreK–3 system. You want to make sure that you have a specific PreK–3 plan that clearly articulates what it will take to build an effective system of support:

- your goals are aligned to your standards or benchmarks,
- your teachers have a consistent curriculum and the tools they require to teach these standards,
- your curriculum implementation is supported by strong professional development, and
- your assessment is aligned to the goals established for the children in your community.

Vertical Alignment

Vertical alignment is the process that ensures that curriculum and standards seamlessly flow from one grade level to the next. This allows the previous teacher and team, as well as the parents, to share all that has gone into the development of the child prior to entering the next learning environment. It enables grade-level teams to capitalize on the successes and learn from any unsuccessful attempts at helping the individual child. The following are vertical-alignment activities that will benefit the child:

- Work with parents to create a "one-pager" outlining the growth that the child has made in all areas of development. Include successful and unsuccessful efforts. Have a parent present this to the next teacher at an orientation meeting.

- Have the receiving teacher start the school year with an inventory of her or his children and families. If you are not able to make individual home visits, have your families work on a family poster during orientation night. Ask families to highlight special interests and gifts that their child and family value.

- Have preschool family advocates arrange a meeting with the families they are working with and the school interventionist or counselor. It is important to do this "hand off" so that families continue to have a supportive person who advocates for their child.

Vertical alignment not only benefits the individual child, but it is an important component to sustaining a quality PreK–3 system of support. We have already provided you with concrete examples of how to align your PreK–3 standards, curriculum, supplemental materials, assessment, and resources. Now have your leadership group inventory the unique strengths of preschool education—the nurturing and strong social and emotional support that is provided to families and children—and make a plan to ensure that this continues through kindergarten and beyond. Find similar services and practical ways to continue the support throughout the grades, and align the academic support with the Early Learning and Development Benchmarks, down to preschool.

"Pass the baton" is a phrase used by many schools and districts to represent the process of "handing off" the students from grade to grade. We have expanded this process to include intentional instructional planning from spring until the end of school to solidify the skills of students in one grade and to include curriculum mapping and adjustment of instruction for the children you will receive in the fall. Here is an outline of this process that ensures you build upon the previous learning and continue to adjust and modify instruction to meet the needs of your incoming children.

In the Fall

• Invite your community preschool partners and kindergarten teachers to a fall celebration. Preschool partners can share what they have been doing to provide children the instruction they require to meet your goals. Kindergarten teachers can take note of what has been done and thank the preschool teachers for all their hard work.

In the Winter

• Display your aligned assessment data to measure the growth that children made from fall to winter. Make sure you include those children at the benchmark level to ensure that they are continuing on the path to success and not slipping back.

• At a public school board meeting, invite preschool-through-third-grade staff and parents to celebrate the children's achievement based on the goals you established and the assessments you aligned. Invite parents who had their child in a preschool-through-third-grade class to provide testimony regarding the quality instruction their child received. A PreK–3 teacher representative can provide testimony on his or her successes, based on assessment data. The school board could pass out certificates of appreciation and invite the press. This process can be initiated with just preschool and kindergarten teachers and parents as your first group of children moves from preschool to kindergarten, building on your success as the children move up through the grades.

In the Spring

• During the first year of your PreK–3 system, invite preschool and kindergarten teachers to an afterschool meeting. Have preschool teachers share with kindergarten teachers what their preschool children know and are able to do as it relates to your goals. Have kindergarten teachers look at their fall curriculum guides and formulate a plan to adjust their instruction based on the children they will receive. Be sure that you do not skip any steps in the curriculum; rather, you may need to adjust the time spent in review or revise the pacing maps for fall instruction. When possible, use a certified trainer knowledgeable in your districtwide kindergarten curriculum to guide your work. Have the trainer work with your grade-level teams to outline what curriculum areas must be covered, where your teachers may need to place an emphasis, and how you adjust your pacing, based on the children you will be receiving. A valuable strategy is to "script out the day" to ensure that all children, districtwide, receive the same quality instruction and opportunity to learn. Prior to the start of school, bring the kindergarten teachers (you may have some new teachers hired at that time) in to review your documented plan and design the first three months of school. Make this document part of each school's comprehensive school improvement plan and post it proudly on your district and school Web site.

• The following year, invite kindergarten and first-grade teachers to a pass-the-baton meeting. Send out invitations with the article "Ladders of Learning: Fighting Fade-Out by Advancing PK–3 Alignment" (Kauerz, 2006) printed on the back of the invitation so that teachers know why they are coming to this meeting. Repeat the process outlined above with other grades. Kindergarten teachers share with first-grade teachers how far their children have progressed; first-grade teachers adjust their plan of instruction based on the strengths of the children they will receive in the fall. The use of a curriculum expert will help teachers design an adjusted curriculum-pacing map to ensure that all critical skills are taught. Then first-grade teachers work together to script out the day, celebrate efforts, and report to the school board and community. Kindergarten teachers work to solidify student skills from the spring to lessen the impact of regression over the summer months.

• Make sure that you track these children, using your aligned assessment plan so that you can follow their progress. Then review, revise, document, and move forward.

The following friendly accountability actions assist in combating the fade-out effect:

- A preschool partnership logo to hang in the window as an assurance of quality instruction and a commitment to working together toward your established PreK–3 goals
- A kindergarten and preschool registration fair to engage parents and publicize your successes
- Monthly or quarterly learning walks: PreK–3 teachers observing in each other's classrooms districtwide
- Media and school board reports to publicize grade-level and PreK–3 success
- Multiple celebrations across grade levels using data to encourage teachers who are working hard to provide children with quality instruction (include measures documenting the growth that children have made)

These are all strategies to build and sustain the gains that your children have made.

There is much to learn from quality early childhood preschool education that will benefit K–12 children and families and especially the K–3 system. It is interesting to interview parents of children who have participated in a variety of programs: birth to age two, age three to age five, and kindergarten to third grade. One parent talked about when her child was in the birth to age two program, teachers and support staff provided services in her home. The plan was based on the strengths and needs of her child as well as the needs of the family. All services, including housing, health, and education, were included in the plan for her family. She attended toddler classes with her child and learned how to extend the learning into her home. When her child entered the preschool system, the child went to school alone, and services were based on the child's individual needs. Her family's access to other services was limited, and it became the family's sole responsibility to locate many of these services. When her child entered the "land of public school," the social and emotional needs of her child took a back seat. The interest shifted to how her child was doing related to academic standards only and in the context of the classroom not the family. She was encouraged to volunteer in the classroom and invited to family nights. However, she felt disconnected from the learning process.

Temporal Alignment

Kauerz refers to the alignment of children's learning experiences within grades and also between grades as *temporal alignment*. She advocates for PreK–3 summer experiences. Step 4 and Step 7 outline instructional practices and support systems that can be used for PreK–3 temporal alignment. Examples include Thinking Maps, positive-behavior support systems, consistent routines and procedures, Recognition and Response at the preschool level, and Response to Intervention at the K–12 level. Additional ways to create temporal alignment include the following:

- Combine your Head Start and Title I resources to develop and implement a preschool and kindergarten summer program.

- Provide summer school intervention as well as prevention by providing children with an extended-learning opportunity using the same successful curriculum or supplemental materials used during the PreK–3 school year.

- Provide opportunities for continued learning outside the school day and between vacations by using community organizations, including faith-based programs. Provide these volunteers with materials that children need to continue their learning. This will align your instruction and maximize the benefits for the children they are reaching.

- Work with your private schools and private tutoring organizations to align your instruction. For example, one of our private faith-based schools goes only through primary elementary; we worked with them to provide the same reading curriculum so children who transfer to public school do not experience a disruption in their learning.

- Work with your before- and afterschool child care programs and Girls and Boys Club to align children's learning experiences. One way to accomplish this at no additional cost is by shifting the workday schedule of your paraeducators or Title I teachers to support before- and afterschool connections with community agencies.

As you are creating a strong PreK–3 system of support that is responsive to the unique needs of your community, make a plan for sustainability.

STEP 8 AT A GLANCE

- Review of specific examples and strategies to combat the fade-out
- Teach the math and reading skills that are developed from birth through age five
- Create specific strategies for the expansion of

  Horizontal alignment

  Vertical alignment

  Temporal alignment

Next Step: Create a sustainable system of support.

Step 9

Create a Sustainable System of Support

You have worked hard to initiate a PreK–3 system of support by connecting your early childhood community with your K–3 system. Do not waste the pain and effort. Build a system that will continue to expand and respond to the needs of the children and families in your community from the start. This requires careful planning on the part of your leadership group along the way. Here are four key components that your group will want to be working on in order to create a sustainable system: broad-based support and financing, celebrating and publicizing your efforts, engaging members inside and outside your community, and planning ahead. As you progress in building your system, reflect and review, taking note of where you are and what more you might want to do in each of these areas. We refer to this concept as *striving for excellence*. You will be working on all areas simultaneously and finding that in each one there are members on your team and throughout your PreK–3 organization that will have specific strengths and established relationships with people in and outside your community. Your core leadership group and "cheerleaders" throughout your community will further your efforts by branching out to state officials, organizations, businesses, and others. Just as you were able to locate and connect with your early childhood preschools, you should build on existing relationships and expand your reach across your state and beyond.

Your community has unique strengths and challenges that your group will want to plan for and address. The hallmark of a powerful PreK–3 system is the ability to continue to grow and provide supports that are relevant to the strengths and needs of the children and families in the community. Using the "Four Key Components of Sustainability" guide located at the end of this section, have your leadership group discuss each component and formulate a plan.

Identify key people who have established relationships or are connected to (know the language of) the group you are trying to reach. When choosing people on your team to take the lead, consider those who have the knowledge and hands-on experience in the area you are developing. Build capacity both within and outside your organization to lessen the dependence on specific individuals. When others start to "catch your vision" and think of ways to expand and build upon your efforts, you will know that you are well on your way to building sustainability.

Broad-Based Support and Financing Your Goals

Continue to build leadership throughout your entire system. Elevate early learning to a level of importance by recognizing and promoting early childhood leaders in your community and throughout your school organization. One explanation for early childhood not being included, or seen as the impactful intervention it is, is that often the early childhood leaders are not at the table for the discussion. Even when representatives for early childhood are part of the discussion, they often lack positions of authority to make decisions. However, an example of being supportive emerged from the Bremerton School District. Then-superintendent Dr. Bette Hyde and the school board elevated the importance of the early childhood efforts by recognizing and legitimatizing the work of connecting the early childhood community to the K–12 system. The Bremerton community's early childhood collaborative effort started 27 years earlier. Yet, it was not until the superintendent, assistant superintendent, and the school board made it a part of the district's goals that the community, followed by the mayor and state officials, recognized Bremerton for its success in working with community preschools. Here are a variety of ways to plan for and establish broad-based support:

• Recognize and legitimize existing efforts at the highest level within your administrative team. For example, if the special programs director or Title I director is leading the charge, make this effort part of the director's weekly duties and responsibilities. Many schools have an administrator who is working on this effort on the side because of the importance of quality early childhood education to student achievement. Write this into the existing duties of that department, giving the director budget authority. Publicize this information for parents and staff on your district Web site and make it part of the end-of-the-year department reporting and planning process.

- Promote early childhood and K–3 staff that are performing leadership roles with a specific title and additional pay if possible. If not, record additional duties as part of their job description, gather positive letters, and include community recognition in their evaluation. Provide additional days dedicated strictly to PreK–3 efforts or a stipend to recognize the work being done. Even without additional funding, a title, position, and adjusted duties are excellent ways to acknowledge the additional work that is being done. When listing your leadership group on your Web site and in your minutes, recognize these people for the early childhood PreK–3 work that they are doing for building your system of support. A title and brief description of what a person is doing allows families and principals to contact the right person. This provides a way for other partnerships to form and expands your community preschools, thus reaching more children prior to kindergarten.

- Encourage your community preschool partners to contact other preschools and in-home child care providers in their area to promote and expand your partnerships. The goal is to support more preschool environments to reach more children with high-quality instruction.

- Your leadership group logo or "quality sign" is another way to sustain efforts and gather new partners.

- Keep the work of early childhood and your child outcome data at the forefront of all discussions regarding student achievement. In community, regional, state, and national forums on education, ensure that quality early childhood and K–3 alignment is an important component of student success.

- Have your leadership group make political connections. Provide your group with PowerPoint presentations, DVDs, and one-pagers, publicizing what you have accomplished using your shared goals and data.

- Meet with your local paper's editorial board and request a section devoted to early childhood.

• Divide the responsibilities and encourage members to serve on local boards and agencies that are making a difference for children and families. Possibilities include: hospital boards, mental health boards, Head Start Advisory, Developmental Disabilities Board, United Way, Regional Head Start, and State Principals Association.

Financing Your Goals Through a Flexible Use of Resources Around a Central Target

As part of your plan to build sustainability, be strategic about financing your goals. One way to do this without additional funding is to share your goals with other departments within and outside the organization. Your job is to find other departments that are working on similar efforts and may have resources to share. Student achievement, early intervention, prevention, support for children and families, extended learning, math, and literacy are all central themes or potential initiatives that may enable you to combine efforts and pool resources. For example, many states now have a math initiative that extends to preschool. Resources may include professional development, materials, and family outreach. Another way to gain financing is to actively share your positive results and seek funding from private corporations, nonprofit organizations, and community members interested in furthering your efforts. In these current economic times, it is much easier to attract funding when a project is specific about its charge (goals) and has the outcome data to prove that it's successful.

Align Your Federal Funding to Support and Further Your PreK–3 Goals

As many of you know, the gift of federal funding comes tightly wrapped with ribbons attached to rules and regulations. Funding is accompanied by accountability. Bring together all the federal program coordinators and locate all federal grants aimed at helping children (students) and families, from birth to age eight. Make a list of all federal mandates or requirements that accompany these programs and locate common requirements. Many times, school districts have a mandate associated with a specific program or grant. For example, Head Start, Early Head Start, Migrant Head Start, and Tribal Head Start all have similar mandates that are found in our K–12 federal programs. Parent engagement and transition are two requirements in all Head Start and Title I programs. However, to do an adequate job, one that will make a measurable difference rather than produce a few sprinkled activities, it requires working together to focus your combined resources on one plan that supports and furthers your PreK–3 goals. Start by looking at federal mandates. For example, parent engagement, transitions, professional development, and demonstrating child outcomes are federally nonnegotiable, with a requirement to demonstrate expenditures in these categories by the end of the year. Providing children with quality instruction as a form of prevention is an expectation in all programs. However, you have the flexibility to choose how to target your resources, provided you use research-based practices focused on the needs of children and have measurable outcomes to demonstrate effectiveness. This gives your leadership group substantial flexibility to target resources where they are needed the most. Most recently, special education has allowed funding for early intervention or prevention under the federal guidelines for Response to Intervention (RTI). This opens the door for children to receive additional practice opportunities that are targeted to what they need prior to being identified as needing special education. Listed below are alignment requirements that will help support your PreK–3 efforts.

An examination of following requirements will help you align *federal* funding with your PreK–3 goals:

- Raise student achievement and measure outcomes in the areas of reading and math: Title I, all federal Head Start programs, Special Education, and Title III all have requirements to demonstrate successful child outcomes using local and state assessment data. Connect your Head Start assessment person with your local school district assessment person.

- Professional development focused on research-based instructional practices: This includes the funding of literacy and math coaches in both preschool and K–12 (Title I, Head Start, Special Education, Title III, Title II).

- Transition from preschool to kindergarten (All federal Head Start programs, Title I): Each program is required to have a plan in place and available for federal review that demonstrates teachers working together to provide a smooth transition for children and their families.

- Purchase instructional supplies and materials to increase student achievement: All federal Head Start programs have this requirement. The Title I, Title III, and Special Education requirement is for supplemental materials that support core instruction.

- Family engagement: All federal Head Start programs, Title I, and Special Education have a requirement to support and involve families in the education of their children.

Align State Funding to Support and Further Your PreK–3 Goals

Examination of following requirements will help you align *state* funding with your PreK–3 goals:

• Raise student achievement and measure outcomes in the areas of reading and math. Every state has funding programs that target the needs of low-income students. These state grants are allocated based on your district's or preschool's poverty index (free- and reduced-lunch count). These programs are designed to provide a variety of interventions and preventions aimed at increasing student achievement in reading and math. In Washington state, it's called the Learning Assistance Program (LAP). Many states have early childhood programs that are separate or are part of the public education system. In Washington state, this is the Early Childhood Education Assistance Program (ECEAP), designed to provide children with quality preschool instruction. State special education funding and state funding for English language development often target low-income populations and have similar requirements to federal programs to raise student achievement.

• Professional development focused on research-based instructional practices: This includes the funding of literacy and math coaches in both preschool and K–12 (Same as federal programs mentioned above).

• Transition from preschool to kindergarten: All state-funded early childhood programs and K–12 state-funded public education initiatives to increase achievement include transition requirements due to the significant impact this has on children. Look at your state's K–12 Web site and take note of what they recommend as the best practices in transition. Look for schools highlighted for their successful transition plans and contact them to determine what funding sources they are accessing.

• Purchase instructional supplies and materials to increase student achievement: All state-funded early childhood programs and state programs that target children who qualify for free and reduced-cost lunch have this requirement.

• Family engagement: This is a major component of every school district and preschool's plan. Contact your school district and state early childhood department to inquire about family engagement and possible funding sources.

Align and Share Local Resources to Support and Further Your PreK–3 Goals

Many local agencies are working on similar goals or are looking for ways to focus their resources and volunteer time to make a difference for children. You might consider the following:

- **Local Faith-Based Organizations:** In our community, one of our local churches raised funds to support our collective efforts. It was the first time in our careers that a private school approached a public school board and donated funds for books and materials to reach more children and families prior to kindergarten.

- **Local Businesses:** It is helpful if your leadership group is able to articulate exactly which parts of your PreK–3 efforts need support. For example, if you are looking for literacy center kits to support preschool and kindergarten efforts, a local business may purchase specific items that it can afford rather than hand over a large quantity of money.

- **Local Organizations:** Have members of your leadership group and school district join your local organizations. This develops relationships and extends your community support. Volunteer to present the exciting things you are doing together. Be sure to share accurate outcome data, making it easier for these groups to support your efforts. Kiwanis clubs, Rotary clubs, Lions Clubs, Girl Scouts, Boy Scouts, and the United Way are a few possibilities.

So far, you have not added additional funding; you have simply aligned, prioritized, and reallocated your federal, state, and local resources around current requirements, mandates, and community goals. By eliminating any duplication, and focusing your efforts, you have gained funding in the areas that make the most difference for your children. Once you have seen the first glimpse of positive child outcome data that proves your combined efforts make a difference for children, share it with your local, state, and national organizations, businesses, and private funders. Many private funders have pulled out of projects because of a lack of effectiveness data. Shepard Barbash, in his article "Pre–K Can Work" (Barbash, 2008), highlighted Bremerton School District and its work with community preschools to provide "rigorous, *data-driven* preschool programs for poor children" as one of two quality programs in the United States that benefit children. This is another reason to prioritize your goals and measure your results the very first year; it provides baseline data that is essential to measure your progress. You can never go back and obtain this baseline data again.

Celebrate and Publicize Your Efforts

Having something to celebrate that proves that you are making a difference and making sure that everyone is celebrating with you are important components of sustainability. The death of any successful effort is taking for granted the challenging work of all involved and assuming that everyone is aware of what you are attempting to do. After you have established concrete evidence that a component of your PreK–3 system of support is making a positive impact in the area(s) that you have chosen, give credit to all the participants, celebrate, record, and publicize.

Celebrate Efforts

Distribute the credit; acknowledge even the smallest effort toward your goals. All of us require a little encouragement. Have you ever received a little card or voice mail thanking you for your efforts or endeavors? The three of us have talked about how that makes us feel and how it reminds us to do this more often for others. Here are some other ways to celebrate that will help you build sustainability. The time to plan and implement this phase is now.

• Hold a "you make a difference" meeting or luncheon. In the fall, invite community preschools to a thank-you luncheon. Take the time to talk about the difference a quality preschool makes in the lives of children. Have one or two of your preschool partners share the benefits of working with the school district on this PreK–3 system-building effort. Share data from your preschool partners. Have a few kindergarten teachers, a principal, and a board member at this lunch to thank your preschools.

• The spring kindergarten and preschool registration is another way to publicize your efforts.

• Celebrate growth and successful benchmarks along the way. For example, celebrate children in class who have increased their vocabularies. Be specific about both the criteria and measurement you use; your baseline data and your progress monitoring need to be consistent.

• Celebrate your successes and honor the work that families do with their own children through a monthly publication. Parenting Matters is an example of a nonprofit agency that supports families and children in our community with a monthly publication (*First Teacher*). Teachers, principals, and preschool providers are all encouraged to put articles in each edition.

• Sign up for local, regional, state, and national conference presentations to share what you are doing and have accomplished, as well as how you achieved your goals.

• Nominate your team, school board, or community for various awards they deserve because of supporting your goals.

Publicize in Multiple "Languages"

What is the language of the people within the organization you are trying to reach? Do you ever feel as if you are speaking a different language when you are trying to articulate the importance of this work and what a positive impact this makes for children? Total immersion in the effort makes it difficult to step away for a moment to consider the listener's "language" and adjust our own vocabulary. It is important for your leadership group to be able to match your message to the listeners without compromising your goals. In this case, multiple repetitions are not helpful if the language does not match the background knowledge and area of interest of the group you are addressing. Sometimes you get only one chance to appeal to your audience, and you will want to put forth your very best for the children. The following is a list of overgeneralizations to illustrate this point. Your group will want to consider these languages when preparing your publications. Have fun with this and get started right away.

• **Dollars (Cost Benefit, Cost Analysis):** This is a language compatible with groups such as funders, businesses, and school district budget people. It may not be that these people prefer talking about money; rather, they are required to consider this major factor when prioritizing resources. They are bombarded with multiple requests for resources.

• **Child Outcomes:** Here we are speaking the language of state and local representatives. Your state officials are interested in data to demonstrate the effectiveness of early childhood PreK–3 efforts. These people must answer to their voters and other interest groups that are competing for funding. Programs that have data to demonstrate their cost effectiveness and their ability to be replicated throughout the state have a high probability for funding.

• **Real-Life Stories:** These represent the language of all of us who care about children. Examples of how your efforts specifically impact the lives of children in an immediate and positive way deliver a strong message of hope and validation. When you are able to tie a real event to your specific goals, you make this language even more powerful.

Immerse your leadership group in the language of others. Start with your primary language (passionate statements as to why you are working together to do this work and what it means to you personally) and add the languages of others. For example, you may talk with groups starting with the statement, "We are all here because we want to make a difference for children." You follow this with several reasons why your PreK–3 system of support is successful, "Let me demonstrate why this PreK–3 system is a smart investment: it's financially sound (include cost analysis), effective (show data and progress on your specific goals), and impactful (include stories of the impact on children and families that have benefited and those who are still struggling in your community)."

Continuous Engagement

Take your passion and turn it into action by engaging other members inside and outside your community. Be clear about your targets (goals) and the established agreements your group has made and recorded before expanding your efforts. Use the steps of building your initial PreK–3 system to expand your group. For example, build on the strengths and relationships that members of your leadership group have already established. Is there a parent in your leadership group who will connect with other parents at the community, regional, and state level? You can expand your group's influence by doing the following:

- Have teachers connect to other teachers in your community, your regional educational school district, and state office of public education.

- Your school board members can expand their influence and share your success with other school boards across the state and at the national level.

- Your local service clubs can engage members at the regional and state level.

- You can make appointments with your local and state representatives. You would be surprised how many of your leadership group members are involved in local political organizations. Many will be interested in what you are doing and want to support your community when you are clear about your targets and what you have accomplished for children.

Table 9.1   Four Key Components of Sustainability Guide

1. Broad-Based Support and Financing Your Goals	2. Celebrate and Publicize
Leadership: elevate early learning to a level of importance by recognizing and promoting early learning leaders in your community and school • Establish mutual respect (e.g., include your preschool partners, director's group, superintendent, and school board members in the planning process, implementation, and celebrations) Finance your goals: Redistribute, reallocate, and focus all funding to target your areas of need and meet your goals • Federal • State • Local	Celebrate efforts • Share the credit, acknowledge small efforts ("infuse every position with importance"—*The Way of the Shepherd*, Leman & Pentak, 2004) • Public PreK–3 events such as kindergarten round-up, PreK–3 kick-off, and school board recognition • Publicize with Web sites, stories of success highlighted in your local paper, flyers, and brochures • Publicize in multiple languages • Dollars: language of funders and businesses • Outcomes are the language of state and local representatives • Real life stories: language of all and builds strong connections for memory • You make a difference: language of community and workers in the trenches Immerse each group in the language of others
3. Engagement	4. Looking Ahead
Passion and goals for a variety of audiences and stake holders Leadership group connect and expand involvement with: • Families • Teachers • School board • Business owners • Your community • Your state Establish agreements and move on	Review, revise, and build on your system of support • Expand your system of support to include PreK–20 • Birth to age 2? • More early childhood partners? • More community college and university connections? What are your next steps?

STEP 9 AT A GLANCE

- Establish broad-based support
- Finance your goals
- Celebrate your efforts
- Publicize your efforts in multiple languages
- Engage and expand your sphere of influence by using the strengths and connections of your leadership group members

Next Step: Review, revise, and extend.

Step 10

Review, Revise, and Extend

What are your next steps? This all depends on your community, their needs, and their success with building your system of support. You may decide that you need to go more in-depth in one of your identified focus areas. For example, there is new information on resiliency and self-efficacy that may strengthen your PreK–3 system of support and benefit children. Are you ready to expand by adding another goal? If you chose literacy and social and emotional needs as your primary focus, what about adding math? If you have a strong PreK–3 system of support for your community, apply the same principles and extend your PreK–3 system to P–3 (adding birth to age three). Have you thought about expanding your outreach to parents and perspective parents? Not all children attend preschool prior to kindergarten. Have you considered the other end of the continuum? Build a P–12 support system and beyond. Connect with your community colleges, technical institutes, and universities to expand the quality of course work and practicum experiences and to increase the number of early childhood teachers graduating with the knowledge and skills necessary to teach our young children and provide each child with a strong foundation in all areas of development. Connecting your postgraduation system to your P–3 or P–12 system will assist you in building a strong, coherent system of support. You must have realized by now that your work on systems building will never be complete. Your system starts with a strong set of core values and a desire to help children, followed by a shared commitment to working toward the specified goals and then "looping back" (review, revise, and extend). Self-reflection is a powerful tool when used to identify the strengths of your system, areas that need adjustment, and to identify the next steps. Take a critical look at your own PreK–3 system of support. A solid PreK–3 system of support is far superior to a shaky P–3. Keep a record of the revisions you have made and why. It is important to note your mistakes and adjustments so that you do not waste the pain. Others will want to learn from your work.

Next Step: Looking Ahead and Planning

Dynamic and successful PreK–3 systems of support have a strategic plan to review, revise, and extend. Here are some examples of questions that you can use with your leadership group to help guide you.

Review Your Goals

- Are they still relevant?
- Do we need to expand or modify them based on children's outcomes?
- If so, what are the next steps?
- Review what has made the difference for children and their achievement in your community. Are you able to quantify your achievement as well as tell the personal stories?

Are We Making a Significant Difference?

- What have we accomplished together for children and families?
- How do we know that we are making a difference? Have we gathered data?
- Are we satisfied with the growth that children are making?
- What other information do we need (if any)?
- How are we maximizing the gains that children have made in preschool and working to align our efforts with kindergarten?
- Is there more that we need to be doing?

Your Leadership Group—Early Childhood Care and Education (ECCE)

- What if the ECCE went away tomorrow?
- What are the benefits of having an ECCE (if any)?
- To you?
- To your program?
- To the teachers or staff?
- To the children and families?
- Do we need to adjust or change anything?

Looking Ahead

- Are we building sustainability?
- Are we staying current in our search for research-based teaching and learning practices?
- Do we have shared leadership?
- Are we publicizing our successes?
- Are there other preschools that we are not reaching that might want to join our efforts?
- Extend and expand your efforts vertically and horizontally. What will be your next project—to increase the quality of PreK–3 instruction or to expand your system of support for the children in your community? Be sure to build capacity as you go so that you do not end up with a small number of exhausted people doing all the work.

Here are two examples of how to apply Steps 1 through 9 to further develop and expand your system.

Example 1

Expand Your PreK–3 System to Include More In-Home Child Care Providers, Parents, Grandparents, Family, Friends, and Neighbors.

Step 1

Establish Need and Common Interests (Children and Families)

- Use the same research and information that you shared with your community preschools and PreK–3 group to establish a common level of understanding. Add your first year's progress data to demonstrate to this new group the difference you have made collectively for children in your community. It is important that you share the goals of your leadership group and the reasons for them with this expanded group. Your goal is to broaden your efforts, not to start over. Begin with a small number of providers and parents to build support and maintain quality.

• Gather your in-home child care providers, parents, and grandparents at one of your elementary PreK–3 schools. Have several round-up meetings, presenting the same information at different times to collect your initial group of in-home providers and families. Ask for a commitment and invite all participants to a meeting at a time that is convenient for the majority. At your round-up meetings, ask participants what time of day and day of the week is best to participate in monthly professional development (problem solving and exchange of ideas).

• Actively pursue a relationship based on mutual respect.

• Make sure that you are creating a group that is part of your PreK–3 system from the start and not creating another separate entity. Acknowledge the fact that children are your priority and create a culture of mutual respect for all child care providers and families, making it safe for people to ask questions and exchange information.

• Continue to differentiate your presentations to meet the needs of your audience.

Step 2

*Connect With Your Early Childhood Learning
Environments (In-Home Child care Providers,
Parents, Grandparents, Family, Friends, and Neighbors)*

• Locate in-home child care providers, parents, grandparents, family, friends, and neighbors. Look for providers and parents who live within the boundaries of your elementary schools. Elementary schools tend to be the gathering place for families and in-home child care providers.

• Locate a person who has already established a relationship with your in-home child care community to lead your group. If possible, choose an in-home child care provider who is part of your leadership group and has participated in your monthly preschool professional development. Choose a leader who has firsthand knowledge and experience providing quality instruction that resulted in measureable benefits to children. Your goal is to move forward and expand your unified efforts to reach more children.

• Gather a core group of motivated and committed individuals and invite them to your first group meeting.

• At your first meeting, reiterate the need, your established goals, and review your commitment. Have your leadership group and established members welcome new members so that all participants feel a part of the larger PreK–3 effort. Select representatives of this in-home group to serve on the leadership group. Establish a consistent monthly professional development time that meets the needs of the majority. This in-home group will be on the accelerated learning track.

Step 3

Make Sure Your In-Home Child Care Providers, Parents, Grandparents, Family, Friends, and Neighbors Are Part of Your Existing Leadership Group and Professional Learning Community

• Include them when you are examining the research

• Build on their strengths

• Share current research on the brain (neuroscience) and child development

• Modify or differentiate the core curriculum by providing activities that are appropriate for the children in their care

• Define what quality looks like in an in-home setting

• Agree on formal and informal assessments that arm the child care provider with valuable information to guide learning or provide additional practice

• Formulate and implement a plan on how to disseminate information to and engage very busy families

Figure 10.1   Wanda Selg-Gonzales, Friends Preschool and Childcare

Step 4

Provide High-Quality Professional Development and the Tools That Parents, Grandparents, In-Home Providers, Family Friends, and Neighbors Want and Need to Provide a Strong Foundation

• Provide monthly professional development at a time that is convenient for everyone; this might be one evening or one weekend day per month.

• At the start of this project, "flex" an existing staff member's schedule to provide support for the in-home provider group and families. This demonstrates to the families in your community that as a school district, you value in-home providers and are serious about your efforts to help children.

• Provide professional development. You may want to shorten the time if you have agreed on evening trainings and provide more hands-on activities for the adults. It is hard to process information after working with children all day.

• Use information provided at your monthly professional development (community preschool trainings) meeting and modify it to meet the unique needs of in-home instruction. The research portion of the training will remain the same. All of you share a common interest in helping children. However, you will want to respond to and meet the needs of your wide range of learners. This may require that you spend additional time on some concepts and less time on others. Keep in mind the tremendous opportunities that these folks have to help children. In most cases, they have an established relationship with the children and have small-group opportunities for practice and extended time. Remind each other of the difference high-quality early childhood education makes for a child. The reverse is also true; extended time spent in poor-quality learning environments has a lasting negative impact on children. By providing families and in-home child care providers with relevant research, materials, and activities that use the best practices in the area of teaching and learning, you have eliminated excuses and increased the potential for a child's positive future.

- Have in-home providers create a portfolio of the programs and activities they have provided over the span of a year. This will become a source of pride and serve to encourage in-home providers to continue to learn and expand their expertise.

- Maintain high expectations for children's learning and focus all conversations on what you are able to do collectively to help children. From the start, set up a productive training that honors people's sacrifice of time away from their homes. Acknowledge that there are a multitude of important issues and needs outside the charge of this group that surround our families and providers. Therefore, set time aside apart from the designated training time to allow people to network and share the resources that your community offers. One option is to include time to exchange at the end of the training session.

- Grow leaders among your group. You want individuals that are willing to be trained and who will provide training to others.

- Provide child care during your monthly trainings.

- Invite child care providers to attend regional and state level conferences.

- Celebrate and publicize your success.

Step 5 and Step 7

Connect and Align Quality PreK to K–3

- Connect your extended group of in-home child care providers, parents, grandparents, family friends, and neighbors to the closest elementary school.

- Include these people in your school activities and events.

- The elementary principal again plays a key role in welcoming families and incorporating their strengths and areas of interest into the school.

- Whenever possible, set up a room for parents in your elementary school.

- Include this group in your assessment and information loop.

- When sharing staff, materials, and other resources, include this in-home group as well.

Step 8

Conquer the Fade-Out

- It is important that you educate your extended group about the possibility of fade-out and inform them of what you are doing to ensure that this does not happen in your community.

- Actively seek ways to include this group in your design and implementation of all the strategic steps.

Step 9

Create a Sustainable System of Support

- This extended in-home group will increase your broad-based support. These folks support your schools and local levies.

- This is the group that will want to celebrate with you and pass the word about the positive impact you are making for children and families in your community.

- Include this group in your strategic plan to review, revise, and extend.

Example 2

Connect With Your Community Colleges, Technical Institutes, and Universities

Expand your P–3 or P–12 system by connecting with your community colleges, technical institutes, and universities to increase the quality and availability of course work and training related to your goals for children. You want to increase the number of first-year early childhood teachers who are ready to meet the challenges of today's children. We desperately need teachers who are knowledgeable about what it takes to teach young children and have the passion and skills to do this important work. When early childhood teachers are competent and successful at the start, and acknowledged for their early learning contributions, they are more likely to stay in the profession. Now you have come full circle in your plan to build a sustainable system of support, one that will continue to respond to the needs of your community and replenish your supply of quality early childhood teachers. It may surprise you that the steps required to include higher education in your support system are similar to the steps used in the initial development of your PreK–3 system of support.

Step 1

Establishing Need and Common Interests (Children and Families)

• Share the research and information you have gathered to establish your need and PreK–3 goals.

• Share the list of reasons that compelled you to unite with your early childhood community.

• Acknowledge the fact that children are also a priority of higher education and technical institutions. Training adults to work with families and to teach children is so important to the work you are doing.

• Actively pursue a relationship based on mutual respect.

• Gather information to share for your first meeting with higher-education personnel. Be specific about your need, goals, and the progress you have made so far.

• Approach higher-education personnel with a call for help. You need this expanded effort to reach more children and sustain the positive gains you have made.

Step 2

Connect With Your Early Childhood Learning Environments

• Connect all the members of your group: representatives from your community preschool teachers, in-home providers, school district K–3 teachers and administrators, and post-high school institutions.

- Inventory how many of your PreK–3 teachers attended these colleges or technical schools and how many are working on continuing their education. You will be amazed at the connections already established.

- Student teachers and interns in your buildings are wonderful resources to locate and connect PreK–3 with higher education.

- At the first meeting, share your established need, create a culture of inquiry and problem solving, and invite all your representatives to join your existing PreK–3 leadership group.

Step 3

Your Leadership Group Now Includes Higher Education

Many of the same strategies outlined in Step 3 apply to the extension of your PreK–3 system of support to include higher education. We believe that one of the important functions of higher education is to provide quality professional development and education that supports your established goals. At times, there may be conflicting views on what and how to teach young children. Stay true to the research that you have examined and your strategic plan to reach your goals. Be sure to articulate the reason your leadership group exists and provide written materials on your agreements and your stand on the issues you have discussed as a group. Invite higher-education personnel to be part of supporting your efforts. If some do not want to join, do not give up. As your PreK–3 efforts pay off in dividends for children and families in your community, others will want to join.

Personally, one author has had positive experiences with several universities and community colleges, jointly designing and teaching associate's, bachelor's, and master's level course work on early childhood education, assessment, and social and emotional development. She has found that many colleges welcome the relevant experiences and practical application that many of us in the field can offer. We appreciate the access to researchers in the field and the wealth of knowledge that many universities and technical schools have to offer.

- Examine the research together and share a common language centered around teaching and learning.

- Build on strengths and inventory the structure already in place to provide adults with a rich learning experience. Inventory what these folks are already doing to prepare adults to meet the goals you have established for children.

- Strive for excellence by working together to design course work and practical experiences that meet the current educational needs of the adults in your community.

- Review your professional development plan to provide all teaching staff with the tools and information they require to meet your established goals.

- Ask higher-education personnel what supportive role they are able to play.

- Share your definition of quality early childhood education and take representatives on a tour of your PreK–3 classrooms. Talk about your successes and your struggles. Tour training facilities and local colleges.

- Share your agreements on assessment and information gathered on PreK–3 children with higher-education personnel. What knowledge and experience do their graduates bring in the areas of curriculum, assessment, and instruction? Thank the universities for what they already provide and ask what their plans are for the future.

- Formulate and implement a plan to support your goals.

- Establish broad-based support to finance your goals and publicize your success.

Step 4

Provide High-Quality Professional Development and the Tools Teachers Want and Need to Do This Work

Professional development is an area that has great potential for collaboration, with both sides playing a supportive role. The University of Florida is a wonderful example of a cooperative effort to provide public school teachers with the ability to further their education for a fraction of the cost, while continuing to work full time in our profession.

- Design professional-development classes, including course work aligned to the goals you established for children and teachers.

- Work together to provide affordable and accessible continuing education and training.

- Meet the needs of a wide variety of learners.

- Provide job-embedded coaching and practicum experiences for course credits.

• Make data gathering, celebrating, and self-reflection part of every class.

• Connect your higher education and training institutions with perspective teachers, support personnel, and instructional assistants in the field of early childhood education.

• Raise the importance of early childhood expertise, training, and education to the highest level.

• Community preschool directors and K–12 administrative staff play an important role by encouraging staff and making it easy for staff to participate in professional development. Sharing resources and funding job-embedded professional development, such as providing instructional coaches and aligning professional development with their school's Comprehensive Strategic Student Achievement Plan are other supports to staff.

• Align higher education with your PreK–3 early learning benchmarks and K–3 state standards.

• Train teachers and support staff on assessment.

• Include knowledge of curriculum, instructional practices, and alignment as part of a teacher's preparation.

• Share, connect, and align resources to support your goals.

Step 6

Maximizing the Benefits of Full-Day Kindergarten

For teachers who have a passion to teach kindergarten, provide the opportunity to earn master's level credit in the area of teaching and learning. Both preschool and kindergarten require extensive knowledge in brain development, social and emotional needs, self-efficacy, language, cognition, reading, writing, math, fine and gross motor skills, and much more. Apply key components of quality instruction to relevant course work, making it easily accessible and affordable to teachers. Often, it is our youngest and least experienced teachers who are placed in early childhood PreK–3 positions, making it difficult for them to continue their education while establishing financial stability. Our children are the ones who benefit most from knowledgeable and experienced teachers.

Step 8

Conquer the Fade-Out

Teachers with knowledge and expertise in the essentials will go a long way toward insulating your PreK–3 system from the risk of fade-out. Make sure that the training and course work provided by higher education and technical institutes addresses the knowledge of instructional practices that build and align your PreK–3 system of support. The following key components of combating the fade-out will need to be explicitly taught and not left up to discovery:

- Alignment of Early Learning and Development Benchmarks with K–3 standards and assessments

- Development of an assessment and information loop

- Alignment of P–3 assessments that includes assessment for and of learning.

- Alignment of core curriculum and supplemental materials

- Use of instructional practices that meet the needs of a wide variety of learners (e.g., Recognition and Response in preschool and Response to Intervention for K–12)

- How to provide optimum learning environments and teach skills in P–3 areas that are necessary for children to know and be able to do

- How to design and implement a plan for horizontal, vertical, and temporal alignment

Step 9

Create a Sustainable System of Support

Higher education and postgraduate training will help you build a sustainable PreK–3 system of support in all the areas covered in Step 9. Make higher education an integral part of your plan for sustainability. Ask for their help and consideration on the following as they relate to your established goals for children:

- Establishing broad-based support

- Financing your goals

- Celebrating your collective efforts

- Publicizing your efforts in multiple "languages"

- Engaging and expanding your sphere of influence by using the strengths and connections of your leadership group members

- Participating in self-reflection and planning the next steps

What will be the next steps in your journey to provide a strong early childhood foundation and to improve the achievement and opportunities for all children in your community? We believe that by examining the steps in this book and modifying them to meet your own needs, you will be able to build a quality PreK–3 system of support that will change the lives of children. We look forward with hope and anticipation to the many children you reach through your collective efforts. Please let us know of your efforts so we can spread the word and share in your joy and celebration.

Resources

Resource A: Books and Web Sites

Classroom Resources

Adams, M. J., Foorman, B. R., Lundberg, I., & Beeler, T. (1997). *Phonemic awareness in young children: A classroom curriculum.* Baltimore, MD: Paul H. Brookes.

Beck, I. L., McKeown, M. G., & Kucan, L. (2002). *Bringing words to life: Robust vocabulary instruction.* St. Louis, MO: San Val.

Blevins, W. (1999). *Phonics from A to Z (grades K–3): A practical guide.* New York: Teaching Resources.

Cummings, C. (2000). *Winning strategies for classsroom management.* Alexandria, VA: Association for Supervision and Curriculum Development.

Florida Center for Reading Research. *Student center activities.* Retrieved from http://www.fcrr.org/Curriculum/SCAindex.htm

Martin, J., & Milstein, V. (2007). *Integrating math into the early childhood clasroom: Actvities and research-based strategies that build math skills, concepts, and vocabulary into classroom routines, learning centers, and more.* New York: Scholastic.

Marzano, R. J. (2004). *Building background knowledge for academic achievement.* Alexandria, VA: Association for Supervision and Curriculum Development.

Sprick, R., Garrison, M., & Howard, L. (1998). *CHAMPs: A proactive and positive approach to classroom management.* Longmont, CO: Sopris West.

Early Childhood

Bowman, B. T., Donovan, M. S., & Burns, M. S. (2000). *Eager to learn: Educating our preschoolers.* Washington, DC: The National Academies Press.

The Center for the Improvement of Early Reading Achievement (CIERA) is a national center for research on early reading. Their Web site is http://www.ciera.org

The National Association for the Education of Young Children. This is a professional organization that promotes excellence in early childhood. Resources and current issues in early childhood are highlighted at http://www.naeyc.org/

National Association for the Education of Young Children. *Developmentally appropriate practice in early childhood programs serving children from birth through age 8.* Retrieved from http://www.naeyc.org/files/naeyc/file/positions/position%20statement%20Web.pdf

National Association for the Education of Young Children. *Where we stand on curriculum, assessment, and program evaluation.* Retrieved from http://www.naeyc.org/positionstatements

National Center for Education Statistics. *Early childhood longitudinal study, kindergarten class of 1998–99 (ECLS-K) kindergarten through eighth grade.* Retrieved from http://nces.ed.gov/ecls/

National Institute for Literacy. *Developing early literacy: Report of the national early literacy panel.* Retrieved from http://www.nifl.gov/

Neuman, S., Roskos, K., Wright, T., & Lenhart, L. (2007). *Nurturing knowledge: Building a foundation for school success by linking early literacy to math, science, art, and social studies.* New York: Scholastic.

Washington State Office of Superintendent of Public Instruction. *Washington State: A guide to assessment in early childhood: Infancy to age eight.* Retrieved from http://www.k12.wa.us/earlylearning.guideassess.aspx

Families

The Florida Center for Reading Research provides grade-level resources and suggestions for families to use at home. Their Web site is http://www.fcrr.org/curriculum/curriculumForParents.htm

Parenting Matters publishes newsletters for organizations focused on families with children from birth through third grade. For more information e-mail website@parentingmatters.org or call toll free: 1-866-943-KIDS (5437).

The Washington Research Institute and the University of Washington have developed a literacy series called *Language is the Key.* Their Web site is http://www.walearning.com/

Leadership

Leman, K., & Pentak, W. (2004). *The way of the shepherd: 7 ancient secrets to managing productive people.* Grand Rapids, MI: Zondervan.

National Association of Elementary School Principals. (2005). *What principals should know and be able to do: Leading early childhood learning communities.* Retrieved from http://www.leadershiplinc.ilstu.edu/downloads/whatprincipalsshouldknow.pdf

Simmons, D. C., & Kame'enui E. J. (2003, March). *A consumer's guide to evaluating a core reading program grades K–3: A critical elements analysis.* Retrieved from http://reading.uoregon.edu/cia/curricula/con_guide.php

Learning Disabilities

Fletcher, J. M., Lyon, G. R., Fuchs, L. S., & Barnes, M. A. (2007). *Learning disabilities: From identification to intervention.* New York: The Guilford Press.

Learning Disabilities International has free resources and research for parents and educators. Their Web site is www.ldanatl.org

Shaywitz, S. E. (2004). *Overcoming dyslexia.* New York: Knopf.

Research

Caine, R. N., Caine, G., McClintic, C., & Klimek, K. J. (2009). *12 brain/mind principles in action: Developing executive functions of the human brain* (2nd ed.). Thousand Oaks, CA: Corwin.

The Center for the Improvement of Early Reading Achievement (CIERA) is a national center for research on early reading. Their Web site is http://www.ciera.org/

ED Pubs. You can order free U.S. Department of Education publications from ED Pubs, Education Publications Center, U.S. Department of Education, P.O. Box 1398, Jessup, MD 20794–1398. Their Web site is http://edpubs .ed.gov/

The Foundation for Child Development provides research, support, and information for those individuals seeking to restructure and improve the quality of PreK–3 education. Their Web site is http://www.fcd-us.org/

National Mathematics Advisory Panel. (2008). *Foundations for success: The final report of the National Mathematics Advisory Panel.* Washington, DC: U.S. Department of Education.

The National Right to Read Foundation. *A synthesis of research on reading from the National Institute of Child Health and Human Development.* Retrieved from www.nrrf.org

Willis, J. (2007). *Brain-friendly strategies for the inclusion classroom: Insights from a neurologist and classroom teacher.* Alexandria, VA: Association for Supervision and Curriculum Development.

Contact

Please visit the authors' Web site at http://www.MakingADifferencePreK3.com.

Resource B: Suggested Outline
for Your First Leadership Meeting

1. Thank your preschools for all that they do for children and families.

2. Provide an introduction to the meeting.

3. Create a presentation on the need for children to enter kindergarten with a strong foundation in all areas of development followed by quality kindergarten–third-grade instruction.

4. Establish broad-based goals grounded in your passion to help children: *vision plus action*.

5. Name your group and establish your next meeting time.

6. Send out follow-up thank-you notes with your new group name, stated goals, list of participants, and next meeting date.

Resource C: Leadership Guide

Reviewing Our Goals and Our Impact on Children

Review Our Goals	Are We Making a Significant Difference?
• Are they still relevant? • Do we need to expand or modify them based on children's outcomes? • If so, what are the next steps?	• What have we accomplished together for children and families? • How do we know that we are making a difference? (Data gathering?) • Are we satisfied with the growth that children are making? • What other information do we need (if any)? • How are we maximizing the gains that children have made in preschool and working to align our efforts with kindergarten? • Is there more that we need to be doing?
Our Leadership (ECCE Group)	**Looking Ahead**

• What if the ECCE went away tomorrow?
• What are the benefits (if any)
  o to you?
  o to your program?
  o to the teachers and staff?
  o to the children and families?
• Do we need to adjust or change?
	• Are we building sustainability?
	• Do we have shared leadership?
	• Are we publicizing our successes?
	• Are there other preschools that we are not reaching that might want to join our efforts?
	• What are the next steps?

Resource D: Curriculum Adoption Form

Critical Elements of Our Preschool Curriculum	
Name of Program Reviewed: _____	
Reviewers: _____	
Critical Elements	*Descriptors*
• 0 1 2 3 4 5	○ ○ ○
• 0 1 2 3 4 5	○ ○ ○
• 0 1 2 3 4 5	○ ○ ○
• 0 1 2 3 4 5	○ ○ ○
• 0 1 2 3 4 5	○ ○ ○
• 0 1 2 3 4 5	○ ○ ○
• 0 1 2 3 4 5	○ ○ ○
• 0 1 2 3 4 5	○ ○ ○
• 0 1 2 3 4 5	○ ○ ○
• 0 1 2 3 4 5	○ ○ ○
• 0 1 2 3 4 5	○ ○ ○

Resource E: Grow and Glow Self-Reflection Form

Name: _____ Date: _____

Areas	Non-use I have not learned about this area yet; or I do not understand it.	Know I know the basic concept and I have tried a few activities.	Show I have used this frequently and still have some questions.	Grow I consistently use this and extend it into other areas of the curriculum. I would like more in-depth information.	Teach I am ready to collaborate and share information with others about this area. My doors are open for other to observe.
Structure					
Children's work displayed					
Well-defined routines					
Smooth transitions					
Learning center scheduled for 45–60 minutes					
Circle time interactive					
Small-group time					
Phonological Awareness					
Rhyming activities					
Alliteration activities					
Segmenting activities					
Read Alouds					
2-3 readings of story					

Areas	Non-use I have not learned about this area yet; or I do not understand it.	Know I know the basic concept and I have tried a few activities.	Show I have used this frequently and still have some questions.	Grow I consistently use this and extend it into other areas of the curriculum. I would like more in-depth information.	Teach I am ready to collaborate and share information with others about this area. My doors are open for other to observe.
Use of vocabulary words					
Open-ended questions					
Use of story extenders					
Print and Book Awareness					
Print-rich environment					
Wall charts for children to read					
Letter wall used					
Discussion about book parts					
Writing					
Writing center					
Writing materials in all centers					
Assessment					
Informally check student's skills often					
Use assessment data to plan lessons					
My Goal:					

Resource F: What to Look for in Early Childhood Centers

Sufficient Time (For learning)	**Precise Targeting** (Services and supports targeted to struggling children and those who need to be challenged)
• • • • • • • • •	• • • • • • • •
Thoughtful Focus (Powerful learning opportunities and activities planned by experienced team of professionals)	**Accountability** (Data used to guide children; this information is used to assist and effectively guide children to the next level)
• • • • • • • •	• • • • • • • •

Resource G: Guide to Four Key Components of Sustainability

1. Broad-Based Support and Financing Your Goals	2. Celebrate and Publicize
Leadership: Elevate early learning to a level of importance by recognizing and promoting early learning leaders in your community and school • Establish mutual respect (e.g., include your preschool partners, director's group, superintendent, and school board members in the planning process, implementation, and celebrations) Finance your goals: Redistribute, reallocate, and focus all funding to target your areas of need and meet your goals at the following levels: • Federal • State • Local	Celebrate efforts • Share the credit, acknowledge small efforts ("infuse every position with importance"—*The Way of the Shepherd*, Leman & Pentak, 2004) • Public PreK–3 events such as kindergarten round-up, PreK–3 kick-off, and school board recognition • Publicize with Web sites, stories of success highlighted in your local paper, flyers, and brochures • Publicize in multiple languages • Dollars: language of funders and businesses • Outcomes are the language of state and local representatives • Real life stories: language of all and builds strong connections for memory • You make a difference: language of community and workers in the trenches Immerse each group in the language of others
3. Engagement	**4. Looking Ahead**
Passion and goals for a variety of audiences and stake holders Leadership group connect and expand involvement with: • Families • Teachers • School board • Business owners • Your community • Your state Establish agreements and move on	Review, revise, and build on your system of support • Expand your system of support to include PreK–20? • Birth to age 2? • More early childhood partners? • More community college and university connections? What are your next steps?

References

Adams, M. J. (1990). *Beginning to read: Thinking and learning about print.* Cambridge, MA: The MIT Press.

American Federation of Teachers. (2008). *Improved early reading instruction and intervention.* Retrieved from http://www.aft.org/pubs-reports/downloads/teachers/reading4pgr.pdf

Auman, M. E. (2003). *Step up to writing.* Longmont, CO: Sopris West.

Barbash, S. (2008). Pre–K can work. *City Journal, 18*(4), 82–88.

Barnett, W. S. (2008, December 12). The early childhood longitudinal study of the kindergarten class of 1998–99 (ECLS-K). *Harvard Education Letter.*

Blankstein, A. M. (2004). *Failure is not an option: Six principles that guide student achievement in high-performing schools.* Thousand Oaks, CA: Corwin.

Bowman, B., Donovan, M. S., & Burns, S. M. (2000). *Eager to learn: Educating our preschoolers.* Washington, DC: The National Academies Press.

Brewster, C., & Railsback, J. (2002). *Full-day kindergarten: Exploring an option for extended learning.* Portland, OR: Northwest Regional Educational Laboratory.

Caine, R. N., Caine, G., McClintic, C., & Klimek, K. J. (2009). *12 brain/mind principles in action: Developing executive functions of the human brain* (2nd ed.). Thousand Oaks, CA: Corwin.

Callender, W. (in press). *Response to intervention: A practical guide for educators.* New York: McGraw-Hill.

Campbell FA, Ramey CT (1989) Preschool vs. school-age intervention for disadvantaged children: where should we put our efforts? Biennial Meeting of the Society for Research in Child Development, University of North Carolina, Chapel Hill, 27–29 April.

Carroll, T. (2008). Education beats incarceration. *Education Week, 27*(30), 32.

Center for Educational Networking. (2006). *NASDSE explains response to intervention.* Retrieved from http://www.cenmi.org/Documents/FocusonResults/FocusonResultsDetails/tabid/79/articleType/ArticleView/articleId/65/NASDSE-Explains-Response-to-Intervention.aspx

Child Trends Data Bank. (2003). *Full-day kindergarten.* Retrieved from http://www.childtrendsdatabank.org/indicators/102FulldayKindergarten.cfm

Cotton, K. (1995). *Effective schooling practices: A research synthesis 1995 update.* Portland, OR: Northwest Regional Educational Laboratory.

Craig-Unkefer, L., McConnell, S., Morgan, T., & Schwabe, A. (2005). *Factors that promote and impede implementation of best practices in early literacy in various early childhood settings.* Minneapolis, MN: Barbara Nicol Public Relations.

Cummings, C. (2000). *Winning strategies for classroom management.* Alexandria, VA: Association for Supervision and Curriculum Development.

ED Pubs, Educational Publishing Center. (2002). *A new era: Revitalizing special education services for children and their families.* Washington, DC: U. S. Department of Education.

Fermanich, M., Picus, L. O., Odden, A., Mangan, M. T., Gross, B., & Rudo, Z. (2006). *A successful-districts approach to school finance adequacy in Washington.* Retrieved from http://www.washingtonlearns.wa.gov/materials/Tab1Doc1EvidenceBasedReportforAC7-18-06_02.pdd

Fletcher, J., Lyon, G., Fuchs, L., & Barnes, M. (2007). *Learning disabilities: From identification to intervention.* New York: The Guilford Press.

Foundation for Child Development. (2008). *Ladders of learning: Fighting fade-out by advancing PK–3 alignment.* New York: Foundation for Child Development.

Fullan, M. G. (2001). *The new meaning of educational change.* New York: Teachers College Press.

Glascoe, F., & Robertshaw, N. (2007). *PEDS: Developmental milestones professional manual.* Nashville, TN: Ellsworth & Wandermeer Press.

Goffin, S., & Washington, V. (2007). *Ready or not: Leadership choices in early care and education.* New York: Teachers College Press.

Graves, B. (2006). *PK–3: What is it and how do we know it works?* New York: Foundation for Child Development.

Gumm, R., & Turner, C. (2004). *90 minutes plus: Demystifying the reading block.* Minneapolis, MN: National Reading First Conference.

Hart, B., & Risley, T. R. (1995). *Meaningful differences in the everyday experience of young American children.* Baltimore, MD: Paul H. Brookes.

Hirsch, E. D. (2003). Reading comprehension requires word knowledge—Of words and the world. *American Educator* (Spring), 10–28.

Horowitz, S., & Whitmire, K. A. (2008, July). Response to intervention for young children. *The State Education Standard,* 38–42.

Hyerle, D. E. (1995). *Thinking maps: Tools for learning.* Cary: Thinking Maps, Inc.

Johnson, E. M. (2006, August). *Responsiveness to intervention (RTI): How to do it.* Retrieved from National Research Center on Learning Disabilities at http://www.nrcld.org/rti_manual/index.html

Kauerz, K. (2005). *Full day kindergarten: A study of state policies in the United States.* Denver, CO: Education Commission of the States.

Kauerz, K. (2006). *Ladders of learning: Fighting fade-out by advancing PK–3 alignment.* Washington, DC: New America Foundation.

Kettlewell, J. (2008). P-16 councils bring all tiers of education to the table. *Education Week, 27*(40), 6–9.

Lee, V. E., & Burkam, D. (2002). *Inequality at the starting gate.* Washington, DC: Economic Policy Institute.

Leman, K., & Pentak, W. (2004). *The way of the shepherd: 7 ancient secrets to managing productive people.* Grand Rapids, MI: Zondervan.

Levin, H. M., & Belfield, C. R. (2007). *The price we pay: Economic and social consequences of inadequate education.* Washington, DC: Brookings Institution Press.

Lizakowski, T. (2005). *Minnesota early literacy training project: Final report highlights.* Retrieved from http://www.cehd.umn.edu/ceed/publications/earlyreport/default.html#issues

Lundberg, I., Frost, J., & Petersen, O. (1988). Stimulating phonological awareness. *Reading Research Quarterly, 23*(3), 263–283.

Lyon, G. R., & Fletcher, J. M. (2001). How to prevent reading disabilities. *Education Matters,1*(2), 22–29.

Martin, J. D., & Milstein, V. C. (2007). *Integrating math into the early childhood classroom.* New York: Scholastic.

Marzano, R. J. (2004). *Building background knowledge for academic achievement.* Alexandria, VA: Association for Supervision and Curriculum Development.

Mead, S. (2007). *Top notch early education must extend to third grade and beyond.* Washington, DC: New American Foundation.

National Adult Literacy Survey. (1992). *National center for educational statistics: Fast facts, family reading.* Washington, DC: U.S. Department of Education, Ed Pubs.

National Adult Literacy Survey. (2002). *National center for educational statistics: Fast facts, family reading.* Washington, DC: U.S. Department of Education, Ed Pubs.

NAEYC. (2004). *Where we stand: On curriculum, assessment, and program evaluation.* Washington, DC: National Association for the Education of Young Children.

NAEYC. (2009). *Developmentally appropriate practice in early childhood programs: Serving children from birth through age 8.* Washington, DC: National Association for the Education of Young Children.

National Association of Elementary School Principals and Collaborative Communications Group. (2005). *Leading early childhood learning communities: What principals should know and be able to do .* Alexandria, VA: National Association of Elementary School Principals.

The National Center for Education Statistics. (2006). *The condition of education 2006: Fast facts family reading.* Washington, DC: The National Center for Education Statistics.

NICHD. (2000). *The report of the national reading panel: Teaching children to read.* Rockville, MD: The Eunice Kennedy Shriver National Institute of Child Health and Human Development.

National Institute for Literacy. (2008). *Developing early literacy: report of the national early literacy panel: A Scientific synthesis of early literacy development and implications for intervention.* Washington, DC: National Institute for Literacy.

National Mathematics Advisory Panel. (2008). *Foundations for success: The final report of the national mathematics advisory panel.* Washington, DC: U.S. Department of Education.

Natriello, G., Pallas, A. M., & McDill, E. (1990). *Schooling disadvantaged children.* New York: Teachers College Press.

Neuman, S. (2003). From rhetoric to reality: The case for compensation for prekindergarten education. *Phi Delta Kappan, 85*(4), 286–291.

Neuman, S. (2007). Changing the odds. *Educational Leadership, 65*(2), 16–21.

Neuman, S., Roskos, K., Wright, T., & Lenhart, L. (2007). *Nurturing knowledge: Building a foundation for school success by linking early literacy to math, science, art, and social studies.* New York: Scholastic.

Obama, B. (2009, April 14). *The state of the economy* [Speech]. Washington, DC.

Olofsson, A., & Niedersoe, J. (1999). Early language development and kindergarten phonological awareness as predictors of reading problems. *Journal of Learning Disabilities, 32*(5), 464–472.

Patrick, D. (2007). *Commonwealth readiness project.* Retrieved from http://innovation3.pbworks.com/f/from+cradle+to+career+governor+patrick

Pew Study. (2008). *One in 100: Behind bars in America 2008.* Washington, DC: Pew Charitable Trust.

Plucker, J. A., & Zapf, J. S. (2005). *Short-lived gains or enduring benefits?* Bloomington, IN: Center for Evaluation and Education Policy.

Rossi, R. J., & Stringfield, S. C. (1997). *Education reform and students at risk: Studies of education reform.* Darby, PA: Diane Publishing.

School Library Journal. (2008). *Study: Most fourth graders can't read at grade level.* Retrieved from http://www.schoollibraryjournal.com/article/CA6607657.html

Simmons, D., Coyne, M., Kwok, O.-m., McDonagh, S., Harn, B., & Kame'enui, E. (2008). Indexing response to intervention: A longitudinal study of reading risk from kindergarten through third grade. *Journal of Learning Disabilities, 41*(2), 158–173.

Simmons, D., & Kame'enui, E. (2003). *A consumer's guide to evaluating a core reading program: Grades K–3: A critcal elements analysis .* Retrieved from http://reading.uoregon.edu/cia/curricula/con_guide.php

Sprague, J. (2004). *Best behavior: Building positive behavior support in schools.* Longmont, CO: Sopris West.

Sprick, R., Garrison, M., & Howard, L. M. (1998). *CHAMPs: A proactive and positive approach to classroom management.* Longmont, CO: Sopris West.

Stanovich, K. (1986). Matthew effects in reading: Some consequences of individual differences in the acquisition of literacy. *Reading Research Quarterly, 21*(4), 360–407.

Takanishi, R., & Kauerz, K. (2008). PK inclusion: Getting serious about a P–16 education system. *Phi Delta Kappan, 89*(7), 480–487.

Texas Education Agency and the University of Texas System. (2004). *3-tier reading model.* Austin, TX: Texas Education Agency and University of Texas Center for Reading and Language Arts.

Torgesen, J. K. (2004). Preventing early reading failure—and its devastating downward spiral. *American Educator, 28*(3), 32–39.

United Way. (n.d.) *Illiteracy: A national crisis.* Retrieved from http://www.readfaster.com/education_stats.asp

van Barneveld, C. (2008). *Using data to improve student achievement.* Retrieved from www.edu.gov.on.ca/eng/literacynumeracy/inspire/research/using_data.pdf

Vaughn, S. (2005). *Interpretation of the 3-tier framework.* Retrieved from http://www.texasreading.org/utcrla/materials/3tier_letter.asp

Washington State Office of Superintendent of Public Instruction. (2005). *Washington state K–12 reading model.* Retrieved from http://www.k12.wa.us/CurriculumInstruct/reading/pubdocs/K-12ReadingModel.pdf

Washington State Office of Superintendent of Public Instruction. (2006). *Using response to intervention (RTI) for Washington's students.* Olympia, WA: Washington State Office of Superintendent of Public Instruction.

Waters, D L. (2009). *Reflecting on reflection in research and teaching.* Retrieved from http://www.learninghistories.net/documents/reflecting%20on%20reflection%20in%20research%20and%20teaching.pdf

Watson, J., & West, J. (2004). *Full-day and half-day kindergarten in the United States: Findings from the early childhood longitudinal study, kindergarten class 1998–1999.* Washington, DC: U.S. Department of Education.

Willis, J. (2007). *Brain-friendly strategies for the inclusion classroom: Insights from a neurologist and classroom teacher.* Alexandria, VA: Association for Supervision and Curriculum Development.

Index

CORWIN
A SAGE Company

The Corwin logo—a raven striding across an open book—represents the union of courage and learning. Corwin is committed to improving education for all learners by publishing books and other professional development resources for those serving the field of PreK–12 education. By providing practical, hands-on materials, Corwin continues to carry out the promise of its motto: **"Helping Educators Do Their Work Better."**